Dress

DRESS

AN ANTHOLOGY CELEBRATING CLOTHES AND STYLE

Edited by *Vogue* India

HarperCollins *Publishers* India

HarperCollins
PUBLISHERS
Since 1817

First published in hardback in 2017 India by
HarperCollins *Publishers* India
A-75, Sector 57, Noida, Uttar Pradesh 201301, India
www.harpercollins.co.in

1 2 3 4 5 6 7 8 9 10

P-ISBN: 978-93-5277-445-6
E-ISBN: 978-93-5277-446-3

Typeset in Goudy Old Style at
SÜRYA, New Delhi

CONTENTS

FOREWORD

This book has been a personal dream ever since we began work on the first issue of *Vogue* India, that was over ten years ago. It's taken us a decade to realize this dream and give it spine, pages and form. But it is my privilege to say we finally did it! As a magazine, we have dedicated ourselves to quality editorials—a space where both the short and long form are celebrated, where words can be provocative, moving and insightful, and even celebratory of both the writers and their stories. We're delighted that this anthology features the works of some of our favourite writers who have contributed in various ways to *Vogue* over the years.

This book would have remained a pipedream if it wasn't for the perseverance and belief of a handful of enthusiasts—I'd like to thank HarperCollins for being our publisher and partner through the bookmaking process, along with Shahnaz Siganporia whose dogged perseverance helped turn my dream into a reality. And a big thank you to Renuka Modi and Megha Mahindru, from the *Vogue* team. Happy reading!

Priya Tanna

Editor, *Vogue* India

INTRODUCTION

'There is much to support the view that it is clothes that wear us, not we, them; we may make them take the mould of arm or breast, but they mould our hearts, our brains, our tongues to their liking.' –Virginia Woolf

Hubert de Givenchy's black evening gown that made Capote's Holly Golightly jump off the page and onto popular iconography; the withered white satins, lace, and silks that cling to Miss Havisham, one of Dickens's most haunting characters; or the labyrinthine ethical debate over Draupadi's sari in one of India's greatest epics. Storytellers have long twisted thread and fabric into characters in themselves or woven them into the subtle nuances of ambience to frame the perfect setting. The role of dress, dressing and even undressing, sparks a segue into stories and histories, in real and imagined worlds. And so, to commemorate ten years of *Vogue* India, we decided to publish our first book that explores the writer's gaze on clothes, fashion and style–by inviting eighteen writers to interpret and celebrate the word 'dress' through poetry, fiction, memoir and essay.

Amitav Ghosh appropriately begins this anthology with a hark back to one of the country's most ubiquitous staples in men's clothing—the humble banyan—from its etymology to its anthropological link to sailors and relationship with India's own rise and fall. While Moni Mohsin looks at another, more controversial staple—the burka. But rather than analyse it through the lens of contemporary politics or political correctness, she looks at histories closer to her, narrating a heart-warming tale of agency and the lack of it through her maternal and paternal grandmothers' choices to wear and not wear the burka.

Taking the theme of asserting identity through fashion forward is Jhumpa Lahiri's sublime tale of introspection in a changing room. Molly Crabapple's illustrated essay that examines artist and style icon Frida Kahlo's relationship with Tehuana costuming and Tishani Doshi's lyrical poetry filled with rich imagery springing to mind a sort of sisterhood created through dresses, both old and new. Plum Sykes, tells us how Christy Turlington and *Vogue* inspired the dress that made her take on the hallowed halls of Oxford University with a renewed sense of empowerment.

From the hyper urban to a fable-like royal world—Kyung-Sook Shin, Kanishk Tharoor, Chandrahas Choudhury and Samanth Subramanian, explore the idiosyncratic bonds between person and dress. S&M, hidden identities and million dollar artefacts—Manu Joseph heats things up with a bit of crime and drama. Abeer Y. Hoque reveals the art of costuming, Rosalyn D'Mello reflects on the art of undressing and Divia Thani uncovers the traveller's wardrobe. Vayu Naidu brings in the diaspora with a nostalgic gaze on India's favourite garment—the unstitched sari and Vladimir Lucien poetically tumbles into the cycles of the washing machine, while Janice Pariat and Meena Kandasamy cast a more critical eye towards the new conspicuous realm of fast fashion and urge for a slowing down, one by recalling the time of small town tailors while the other looks at recent history and headlines.

This is a labour of love put together with some of our favourite writers moving away from the relentless coverage of style and trends, and immersing instead in individual worlds where fashion breathes another life. And a reminder that every now and again a dress is more than just a dress. Here's *Dress: An Anthology Celebrating Clothes and Style*, *Vogue* India's first book and we hope you enjoy reading it as much as we enjoyed putting it together.

Shahnaz Siganporia
Associate Editor, *Vogue* India

Confessions of a Banyan Addict

Amitav Ghosh

No other garment lies closer to the heart of the Indian male than the banyan. Yet, despite its hundreds of millions of adherents, the ubiquitous under vestment of the subcontinent gets little attention and even less respect: designers scorn it; dudes despise it; its mere outline, were it to be glimpsed, would bring ruin upon an aspiring male model.

I confess that I, like most of my countrymen, am deeply attached to the humble banyan: like many of my fellow devotees, I have never been able to rid myself of the illusion, fostered in earliest childhood, that my banyan provides a necessary layer of insulation without which my shirt would not be dry and my chest would be defenseless against all the germs, viruses and malign tumours that seek to invade it. But reason alone cannot explain the addict's attachment to this garment. For a true devotee the banyan is much more than a mere article of clothing: at the deepest level it is a marker of identity, a link with the past. This is why it annoys me when marketers attempt to rebrand the banyan as a 'sleeveless undershirt', 'singlet' or 'vest'. To call it anything other than a banyan is to demean and disparage a garment that has every right to be proud of its distinctive name and lineage.

The destiny of a word can sometimes hinge on a tiny shift of emphasis. Notice how the word banyan, when it refers to a humble article of clothing, is pronounced with the stress on the last syllable—banyán. Move the emphasis to the first syllable—bányan (as in banyan tree)—and we have a word that is infused with spiritualism and freighted with overtones of ecological benevolence: a word so eminently fashionable, in fact, that hundreds of thousands of products, from soaps to spas and restaurants, have incorporated it into their brand names. Indeed, it may well be one of the most popular brand names in existence: a brief googling produces more than four million entries.

The words bányan and banyán may appear to be as unlike in their fortunes as prince and pauper, but they are actually twins and share exactly the same parentage: both are derived from the name of a well-known Indian merchant community—'bania'.The transition from 'bania' to 'banyan' began some eight or nine hundred years ago, the process being set in motion by Arab and Persian travellers and scholars, some of whom used the word *baniyân* as a generic term for Hindu merchants (the final consonant 'n' was probably added to indicate a collective noun). When Europeans arrived in the Indian Ocean, they adopted the Perso-Arabic usage, and 'banyan' became a general term for things associated with India: the banyan tree is thus merely the 'Indian tree'. In matters of costume, similarly, the word 'banyan' probably once referred to an item of clothing that was distinctive of India. This may have been an ancestor of a vest like those that Mahatma Gandhi used to wear—but it is hard to know for sure, because nothing could be more unlike the Mahatma's simple *angarkha* than the earliest surviving examples of the garment that went by the name 'banyan'. Several of these, dating from the late eighteenth and early nineteenth centuries, are on display at the Victoria and Albert Museum in London: they are sumptuous, heavily embroidered ankle-length robes that look like ornate dressing gowns. They were typically worn by nabobs—that is to say, Britons who had made their fortunes in India.

But these were not the only banyans in use at that time: there was another such garment, just as unlikely as the nabob's robe. No less an authority than Admiral W.H. Smyth, the nineteenth century's pre-eminent expert on nautical terms and usages, was to define this incarnation of the banyan as 'a sailor's coloured tunic'. In other words, at this stage of its evolution, the banyan was a prototype of the modern T-shirt and was usually worn by sailors. It was often accompanied by an accessory that was also of Indian descent: this was the *bandhna*, a headscarf that came to be absorbed into Western costume as the 'bandana'.

How did a sailor's tunic come to be domesticated as our beloved Indian banyan? I believe the transition was effected by lascars—the Asian mariners who formed a large part of the sea-going workforce in the age of sail. These sailors may have been underpaid, but they were the earliest avatars of the global Indian and it is easy to understand why their attire might have possessed a certain kind of glamour in the eyes of their compatriots. It may be difficult to imagine that the humble banyan was ever invested with the same cosmopolitan appeal that would later lead to India's fervent adoption of blue jeans, but it is worth remembering that denim too has returned to the subcontinent after travelling a similarly tortuous route: its colour came originally from an Indian product, indigo, and a common type of clothing made from this fabric took its name from a part of Mumbai–'dungarees' are, after all, natives of the erstwhile Dongari Killa, where the offices of *Vogue* India are now located.

Thus did the 'banyan' (in the original sense of 'Indian') come full circle, having been reshaped and refashioned by a journey across the oceans. In my novel, *Sea of Poppies*, there is a character who has a theory about the banyan: he argues that the status of this garment has risen and fallen with the fortunes of the Indian subcontinent. When India was a land fabled for its riches, the word banyan was associated with extravagantly sumptuous robes; as the subcontinent's fortunes declined, the banyan dwindled into the humblest item of everyday wear. The implication of this, of course, is that as India's economy grows, the fortunes of the banyan will rise again, perhaps to a point where it will become, once more, a finely crafted garment. Designers take note: there is no article of Indian clothing that has a richer, more varied and more cosmopolitan past, and a vaunted place in history awaits the artist who can claim authorship of the next stage in the evolution of the banyan.

Her Place in the World

Moni Mohsin

Fourteen-year-old Tahira pressed her foot down firmly on the paper. She knew from experience that it didn't pay to do otherwise. 'Give me an extra half inch at the front,' she ordered the maid crouching at her feet with a pencil, in readiness to draw the outline. 'Last time you made it too small. My toes were rubbed raw,' she grumbled.

This, the ordering of shoes was a protracted affair. The maid would trace her young mistress's foot and hand the paper to the old munshi outside in the men's section of the haveli, who would deliver it safely to the cobbler who, in turn, would fashion the shoe from the softest calf leather and hope that it met with approval. It would have been easier for all concerned if Tahira, like other women in the village, went to the cobbler herself and let him measure her feet. But Tahira Begum was not like other village women. The eldest daughter of the wealthiest landlord in the village and keeper of its Sufi shrine, she was not allowed to appear before a man unrelated to her by blood, let alone handle her bare feet. Unlike her brother, Tahira Begum had never picnicked in her father's fields or gone hunting with hawks or ridden a horse. She had not even visited the village bazaar or bought a samosa from a street stall. For the truth was that Tahira Begum's life was one of confinement.

Both my grandmothers, Tahira Begum and Mubarik Begum, were born into purdah. Neither of them went to school. They were both literate but whatever little education they came by was acquired at home. They married while still in their teens to men chosen by their fathers—Tahira, my father's mother to her uncle's son and Mubarik, my mother's mother to a man she only saw on the day of her wedding. For the better part of their lives, my two grandmothers lived behind high walls—Mubarik Begum, in the old city of Lahore and Tahira Begum, in her ancestral village of Shergarh, some seventy miles south of Lahore. The only men allowed into their presence were close family members: brothers, fathers, uncles, cousins and perhaps an ancient family retainer. The two women spent their days sequestered in the zenana of their havelis, attended to by serving women. Even their windows did not look out onto busy streets, but into quiet, internal courtyards. On the rare occasions that they ventured out, mostly to visit female relatives, they shrouded themselves in a burka.

My maternal grandmother's burka of choice, if *choice* is the right word, was a biscuit-coloured silk shuttlecock with a crocheted grille over the eyes that allowed her to see out while obscuring her face from the gaze of passers-by. Tahira Begum favoured a two piece—an ankle-length, coat-like garment in black crepe with buttons down the front, teamed with a separate head piece, a large scarf—a little like the head gear worn by the Irish nuns at my convent school in Lahore—that reached almost to the waist and tied with strings under the chin. She viewed the world through a black chiffon veil attached to the headpiece, that she lowered to cover her face. It was only when they were in the safety of a zenana—either their own or that of the respectable homes they were visiting—could they remove their burkas. All the ladies in their families led similar lives.

My grandmothers lived these cloistered lives because they were privileged. Both Tahira Begum and Mubarik Begum were born into affluent families that did not need their women to earn. Their menfolk could afford to segregate them. Purdah, therefore, was more a public declaration of status and economic security in this patriarchal society than an avowal of religious orthodoxy. Had they been born into the modest homes of, say, sharecroppers or cattle herders or domestic servants, they would have had to work alongside their men in fields, pastures and other people's homes to make ends meet. In fact, during the 1930s in Punjab, it was not just Muslim women who observed purdah, but their Hindu and Sikh counterparts too. Among elites, it was the cool thing to do.

I was not born into purdah. By the time I came along, the custom had withered away. Of my two grandmothers, the first to shed her burka was Mubarik Begum. She had the advantage of living in the city, where change came sooner than it did to remote hamlets. In any case, her seclusion had never been as complete as Tahira Begum's. She had enjoyed society; old denizens of the walled city, her family had a wide circle of friends sprinkled around the bazaars and alleys of

Lahore. The ladies of these families would visit each other's homes at weddings, births, funerals and Eid. To make a social call in the neighbourhood, they might don their burkas and flanked by chaperoning maids, sail out on foot. A longer journey necessitated the use of a curtained tonga in which they sat in their burkas.

Tahira Begum, who lived in the only big house in the village, had no such diversions. Aside from her cousins who resided in a wing of the haveli, there was no other society in the village. The only change of scene she ever had was the annual trip to her mother's clan in a village near Multan. Other than that, and perhaps the once-in-a-blue moon visit to Lahore for a wedding, she was confined to the haveli in Shergarh.

In the crammed alleys of Lahore's walled city, propinquity had enforced conformity to the old ways. But when they moved to the modern British-built suburbs beyond, Mubarik Begum and her daughters escaped the gaze of their neighbours and the judgement of their peers. Here, in the sprawling bungalows of British Lahore, the ladies of my mother's family got a faint whiff of freedom, of novel possibilities. The new architecture allowed a new lifestyle, a new sensibility. Houses, set far apart, were now enclosed by hedges and had vast gardens, often spread over three or four acres. My grandmother could grow vegetables and keep a cow. My mother and her older sister played cricket and rounders with their male cousins. They learnt to cycle and raced each other on the circular driveway of their home. The most revolutionary aspect of these modern houses was that they had no separate zenana wings.

Mubarik Begum was the wife of a businessman who made his fortune as a private contractor to the army during the war. He had many Muslim, Sikh and Hindu associates, fellow entrepreneurs with whom he had dealings. Some had become family friends. My grandmother did not sit at the head of my grandfather's dinner table and make polite conversation with his guests, but she did meet some select colleagues who had become family friends. Her daughters, however, were free to meet everyone.

Mubarik Begum had not received a formal education. But she had a lively intelligence and an intellectual bent. She died when I was six, but I have an abiding memory of her sitting cross-legged on her charpai, poring over an Urdu newspaper. She loved poetry and history and read widely. She could recite vast tracts of Ghalib and Waris Shah from memory and loved Sarshar's *Fasana-e-Azad*. Possessed of a vivid imagination, she had a natural flair for storytelling and an unerring feel for the vivid phrase. She called her pillow her raazdar, the confidant, her mattress wafadar, old faithful, and her quilt, ghamgussar, sharer of sorrows. In another age, she could have been a woman of letters, perhaps editing a literary magazine or even hosting a literary salon, fizzing with intellectual heft and witty repartee.

My mother's elder sister, then in her late seventies, once shared with me a childhood memory. One cold December evening in the 1930s, she was alone with her mother in their baithak, or sitting room. They sat on a rug on the floor leaning against large satin covered cushions (gao takias) warming themselves from the heat of a coal-burning brazier. My aunt, then six or seven, was curled in her mother's lap. There was a knock on the door and a visitor was shown in. It was Dr Iqbal, the great Urdu poet and a family friend. He was old then, but his mind was still pin sharp. Swaddled in a large woollen shawl, he lowered himself stiffly to the floor, across the brazier and embarked on a long animated discussion with Mubarik Begum about literature, laced with some politics and gossip. They conversed for what seemed to my aunt forever, their conversation punctuated by bursts of laughter.

While the family still lived in the old city, Mubarik Begum sent her two eldest daughters to school. Victoria Girls High School was a girls-only establishment housed in an old haveli. There were no playing fields so there was no sport or (God forbid!) drama, but it did offer my aunts an education outside the house. My grandmother was keen that her daughters should not miss out on the opportunities that she had not received. In the larger cities of the Punjab, times were changing and so were attitudes. From the late 1930s, the ladies of my mother's family began to go on excursions to Kashmir and Bombay and Calcutta and Rangoon. Their horizons expanded. When my mother and her elder sister (the youngest two of a brood of five sisters) were admitted to a school, it was to a 'modern' institution.

Purpose built, Queen Mary's sat in a huge compound

and was presided over by a progressive English headmistress who put great emphasis on sport, drama, art and music. Here the girls learnt public speaking, Shakespeare, biology and geography. The school even had a pool, where my mother, dressed in a scarlet one piece, learnt to swim and dive. My eldest aunt's daughter became a champion sprinter and participated in athletic meets in pre-Partition Lahore. Unlike many middle-class girls who would whizz around Lahore on their bicycles, my mother and her sisters travelled more sedately in a car. But at least it was devoid of curtains.

Mubarik Begum did not abandon her burka in a grand symbolic gesture. She just wore it less and less frequently so that the only time she actually made a point of donning it was when she went to visit her parents back in their old haveli in Bhaati Gate. After Partition, it became rare to see a lady from a well-to-do household in a burka in the city. But though she had relinquished her burka and was free to come and go as she liked, Mubarik Begum did not embrace a modern lifestyle. She did not go to mixed dinner parties hosted at the homes of my grandfather's business associates. She did not take up golf or cards or go to the races, as some in her class, including her daughters were doing. She never learnt to speak English or acquired a taste for Western food. She continued to live as she always had—as the traditional matriarch of a vast family. And though she continued to take an interest in history, literature and current affairs, she never published her scribblings. Unread, unsung, they died with her.

For Tahira Begum, the transition was not so swift–it took her much longer to discard her burka. A few years into their marriage, my grandfather chose to quit Shergarh. His younger brother was sickly and he decided that he needed the benefits of space and fresh air. Accordingly, the family moved six miles away to a pleasant water-fed parcel of land he had inherited, where he built a house surrounded by open fields of wheat, rice and sugar cane. As at Shergarh, the family compound was still enclosed by walls, but unlike Shergarh, it contained a large garden within and endless fields without. And there were no neighbours. Free at last from the demanding scrutiny of her mother-in-law and the nosy intrusion of the rest of her extended family, my grandmother lived in her own space among tall neem, laburnum and ber trees. The house had a beautiful rose garden and jasmine bushes and best of all, two pet peacocks that minced about in the front lawn. My grandmother loved her peaceful garden and spent several hours of the day there. For her, this was freedom.

Tahira Begum did not have any daughters. Her two sons were at a boarding school in Lahore, where her husband had also been educated. He was an erudite man, my grandfather. A keen reader, he was fluent in Persian, English, Urdu and Punjabi and devoured the literature of all four. When he was not out and about seeing to his land and dealing with tenants, he was reading. Having not had the advantage of a formal education, nor indeed, exposure to the outside world, Tahira Begum did not have recourse to such consolations. It was a lack she felt acutely throughout her life. She must have been lonely but a devout believer, she devoted herself, instead, to prayer. On summer evenings, we'd find her in her garden on her old daybed, deep in prayer under a star-laden sky. A widow for many years, she acquired self-sufficiency and serenity. Solitude held no terrors for her.

Tahira Begum's burka was a symbol of all that she had been denied. It had prevented her from receiving a proper education, from travelling and from widening her circle of friends and acquaintances. Later in life, when she had long shed her burka, she would visit Lahore to spend time at her sons' homes. She would attend mixed gathering there, lunches and sometimes even dinners, but though always dignified, she was reserved around men, not knowing quite how to converse with them or indeed about what.

With the exception of one aunt who wed a cousin, my mother's sisters were all married into feudal families in the Punjab. Their husbands' families were traditional folk whose women observed purdah. My mother, when brought as a bride from Lahore to Shergarh in 1955, had to don a chaadar. A voluminous shroud-like garment in black crepe, it covered her from head to foot. She put up with the chaadar when visiting Shergarh, but when my grandfather complained to Mubarik Begum that his daughter-in-law did not cover her face, my grandmother promptly had a chiffon flap sewn into her chaadar. (You had, in those days, to keep your daughter's in-laws sweet.) But it is instructive to note that it was not

Tahira Begum who complained about her daughter-in-law's bare face. In any case, my mother did not oblige.

'I'd hold my fan in front of my face or sometimes an open book,' she said. 'But I never lowered that flap.'

My sister and I did not have to wear a burka or even a chaadar. Times had changed by the time we came along. Farmers, businesswomen, philanthropists, my mother and her sisters led busy, active lives. Mubarik Begum passed away when I was a child but Tahira Begum lived on until my sister had married and become a mother and I had graduated from university. In all those years, not once did Tahira Begum ever chastise us for our cropped hair, our uncovered heads, our fashionable clothes, our argumentative natures. When we were teenagers, my parents decided to send us abroad for schooling. When we returned as graduates from a British university, our grandmother marvelled at our degrees, at our familiarity with the English language, with our ease in society. Later when my sister wanted to marry out of our caste, many older members of my family were appalled. And had no compunctions about airing their views. But Tahira Begum held firm.

'The girl is demanding her right,' she told my father quietly. 'You cannot deny her her right.'

My grandmothers were not without power. Tahira Begum was knowledgeable about farming and asked astute questions and gave useful advice. Mubarik Begum was the matriarch who advised and guided her children even when they were managing companies and running election campaigns. Both were forceful women who did not shy away from expressing their opinions, even when they diverged from their husbands'. In their homes, both held sway and led busy, useful lives. They were no pushovers but given the opportunity, they could have been so much more.

Because of the history of my grandmothers—particularly that of Tahira Begum—I have always thought of the burka as a repressive garment. I associate it with physical confinement, with social exclusion and with denied opportunities. My father, who had seen his mother's longing for an education at close hand and the thwarted lives of his aunts, founded a girls' school in Shergarh some forty years ago.

Last year I visited the school to meet the fifteen-year-olds who were then in their final matriculation year. I walked into the classroom and my heart sank. Though it was not part of the uniform, every single girl in that room was wearing a black hijab. On my previous visits to the school it had not been so. Perhaps one or two girls in a classroom of twenty might have worn one.

The hijab is clearly not the burka. It does not conceal the face or obscure the body. Nor does it erase a woman's presence from public space. Yet it makes a statement about feminine demureness that I thought was at odds with the purpose of the school which, aside from providing knowledge, was to inculcate self-confidence and a can-do attitude.

I knew that their mothers, ordinary rural women, wives of farmhands, shopkeepers and small tradesmen, did not wear the hijab. They wore traditional dupattas, gauzy scarves loosely draped over the head, leaving the throat—and indeed much of the head—bare. So why then had these educated, young women embraced a garment that to me was a symbol of women's oppression? Struggling to contain my dismay, I asked them what they intended to do after completing school. They all wanted to study further.

'And then?' I asked.

Twenty-two eager hands shot up.

'Miss, I want to do accountancy.'

'I want to be a pharmacist.'

'My dream is to be a pilot, Miss.'

'I want to be a computer programmer.'

'I want to do doctory.'

'I want my own beauty salon.'

Long after I returned from Shergarh, my head was in a whirl, trying to process the disjuncture between what I had just seen and heard. These were enthusiastic, confident young girls eager to test their mettle in a competitive, mixed work place. Their minds were not limited by other people's constraining notions of their abilities or roles. Unlike students from years past, their ambitions went well beyond traditional 'female' jobs—teacher, nurse, health visitor. So why then were they in hijab?

And then two thoughts occurred to me. When we had conversed, I had spoken in Punjabi, they had replied in Urdu. In rural Punjab, Urdu is seen as the language of town people, of educated classes, people who work in air-conditioned offices, not sweltering fields. It is not the language, they think, of peasants, but of white-collar workers, of the middle class. So when Punjabi villagers make it a point to speak Urdu, they are making a statement about their social aspirations and economic class.

When a woman chooses a hijab over a dupatta, she is making a similar declaration about her place in the world. The hijab is not an indigenous garment but a Middle Eastern import. The Middle East is, in many people's imagination and indeed experience, a place of economic opportunity. Rural families who have sent a son to Dubai, Bahrain or Jeddah, have prospered on his remittances. They have gone up in the world, entering the middle class within a matter of four or five years. Dubai and Abu Dhabi are also perceived as sophisticated, glamorous places with their skyscrapers, snazzy cars and glittering malls. So, when a girl in a Punjabi village dons a hijab, she is distancing herself from her dupatta-wearing mother who probably works on the land. Instead, she is positioning herself as an educated young woman with professional ambitions that will secure her a life of urban, middle-class respectability.

As the burka was a symbol of social status for women of Tahira and Mubarik Begums' generation, so is the hijab for many young women today. But the crucial difference between then and now is that my grandmother's burkas were imposed, while the girls' hijabs express their own choices. My mother and aunts discarded the burka to step into the world. Their daughters, in turn, went on to become educationalists, diplomats, politicians, vets, journalists and activists. But there is no doubt in my mind that the girls from Shergarh, who willingly adopted the hijab, will go on to become accountants, pharmacists and doctors and pilots. And I cannot wait.

A Boy in Uniform

SAMANTH SUBRAMANIAN

For a dozen years, my wardrobe was occupied chiefly by the uniforms it held: three sets, one after the other, for the three schools I attended. Other clothes were secondary—ragged T-shirts and shorts to wear out to play or at home, and the stray decent shirt, with a collar and perhaps even long sleeves, to slip into on semi-formal occasions. (There weren't many.) For a third of the year, roughly speaking, the school uniform was my default appearance. This is, of course, the case for anyone who went to a school that required a uniform. But there cannot be too many other people whose sense of couture, well into adulthood, continues to be defined by the uniforms they wore a decade or more ago. My wardrobe today betrays that readily—gives up, like a weak criminal under nasty interrogation, the fact that I have never really learned how to dress for my post-school life.

Ironically, perhaps the nattiest I've ever been dressed was in my first uniform, at a school in Delhi. During winter, little boys were instructed to wear Lincoln green blazers, grey sweater vests and grey woollen trousers, white shirts, and green ties; girls switched out the trousers for skirts. At assembly, from the stage, we must have looked like one giant rock covered with moss. The school shop sold two types of ties: the regular kind and the kind with a band of elastic that you could just clip under your collar. Regrettably, I chose the second: I was lazy and I didn't think I would ever grow up, so I reckoned that knotting a tie was an unnecessary hassle. Even today, I leave my ties pre-tied; at best, I might undo one, summon up a YouTube video and tie it up again in front of a mirror. In this regard, I am in no way my father's son.

One of the first set of books I ever read starred a boy wearing a very similar uniform. In Richmal Crompton's rich and gloriously funny Just William series, her schoolboy hero—Mister William Brown, as he sometimes introduced himself—was clothed in a blazer, a tie and a sweater-vest, and in shorts, knee-high socks and black shoes. Additionally, he had a school cap, a shallow dome of cloth that sat askew upon his spiky hair. For William, the uniform was something to be fought against. He swung his blazer over his head, muddied his boots and allowed his socks to pool around his ankles. He found alternate utility in some items: he filled his cap with water so that he could carry tadpoles and little fish and he deployed his tie as a makeshift slingshot. His pockets ripped at the seams because they bulged with stones and hard-boiled sweets. Every morning, he was sent to school with a shining face and tidily combed hair; every evening he returned, encrusted in grime, mud and happiness. The entropy of the uniform corresponded to a rise in William's well-being. The very essence of boyhood rebellion was captured in the way William treated his uniform.

Even at William's age, though, I never regarded the

uniform and its various discomforts as any sort of imposition; there are, within the Indian schooling system, only so many forced discomforts you can balk at before wearying of the endeavour. Putting on a uniform was a thing to be done, just as going to school was a thing to be done, as was completing homework, brushing your teeth, or submitting to a bath. Outside of fiction, a child quickly discovers how limited his agency is, and recognizes just as swiftly the parts of his life that are non-negotiable. He reserves his energy for smaller contests that might potentially be won. Inexplicably, that wisdom in picking battles wanes, rather than waxes, with age and time.

In India, the modern uniform is a cultural imposition as well—yet another artefact of British rule. We have no detailed information about what children in precolonial India wore to school; *pathshalas*, *maktabs* and *madrasahs* presumably had dress codes, signals to distinguish the scholastic world from the temporal. The oldest school uniform in England today is the one worn by pupils at Christ's Hospital, a school in Sussex: mustard-yellow socks, a brown leather belt, a white shirt and a long coat that looks as if it was nicked from the stores of a wizarding academy. This 'Tudor look' has been the school's regulation attire for more than 450 years; since 1987 though, Christ's Hospital admits, a streak of anarchy has crept in, and 'Dr. Martens have [become] the perfect accompaniment to the Tudor uniform.' The shades of blue and yellow were chosen, in part, because those dyes were inexpensive; Christ's Hospital was a charity that gathered up 'fatherless and poor children', cared for them, and educated them. The fee to send a child as a boarder to Christ's Hospital today runs to around £10,500 per term.

The impulse to clothe these foundlings and waifs identically was an understandable one. They came into the school with few material possessions of their own, in any case; the uniform was a symbol of leaving the misery of their previous lives behind, as well as a method to knit the students together into a shared new life. Those reasons had also created the academic uniforms of another, earlier sort of student–not a child in school, but a novitiate monk. Hence the robes: two pieces of unstitched cloth for the young men in Vedic *pathshalas*, the orange cloth swaddling Buddhist monks as they moved between the eight lecture halls of Nalanda, the coarse habits of the Carthusians, the Benedictines and the other residents of the great, hushed monasteries of Europe. The robes shredded vanity and dissolved differences; they turned the mind upon itself, away from matters of the external world.

I was grateful for the anonymizing power of uniforms when my family moved to Jakarta, just as I was entering the fourth grade. My sister and I were enrolled in an international school, because expat children weren't permitted–as far as I remember–to attend regular Indonesian schools. Our uniforms: batik shirts, in blue and black for junior school, and grey and black for senior school; dark blue shorts or skirts. We had, furthermore, a separate kit for physical education: white, collared T-shirts and baggy shorts made of some Klein Blue synthetic that I came to detest. The very notion of changing clothes in school—not to mention the compulsory showers after games—was utterly alien. A fine way to discomfit a sheltered Indian boy in the earliest throes of puberty is to strip him and shove him into a communal shower hall with dozens of his naked peers, nearly all of them taller and broader than him.

In other ways too, this school was an unfamiliar universe. The boys were devotees of different music, watched different things on television, played different sports on weekends. When we met outside of school, they wore intriguing T-shirts emblazoned with the names of bands—not just bands, but bands they knew well and had listened to, a connection between leisure and leisurewear that had never existed in my conceptions. These were not feats I could pull off. I owned three audio cassettes, all bequeathed to me—along with her tastes—by a cousin, and most of those musicians didn't feature on T-shirts. I loved to read, but nobody was making streetwear feat. Richmal Crompton or characters out of the Soviet Union's Raduga Publishers' books; I'd seen a lot of Doordarshan but only one-and-a-half English movies, the half because my father dragged me out of *Coming to America*, realizing it wasn't quite right for a seven-year-old; again, these experiences were never quite captured by decals on fabric. My batik shirt, though, looked exactly the same as the ones worn by my Australian friends. For them, clothes were ways to express their individuality; for me, clothes offered a ruse to blend in. The uniform was a profound source of comfort.

I remember none of this, I should mention, as a distressing experience, or even one that troubled me consciously. I adjusted the way most children adjust: honestly and without deliberation, acquiring new aspects to myself and sanding down old ones. But I did indulge in one trick for a year or so, which may now be revealed in these pages.

Jakarta was hot and humid; you always wore perspiration next to your skin. Our classrooms were air-conditioned, and the constant alternation between the bone-chilling indoors and the sweaty outdoors triggered (or so doctors and my parents believed) frequent colds and subsequent asthma attacks. One of these doctors suggested that it might be a good idea to wear a singlet—a good, old-fashioned Indian banyan—below my shirt, as a sort of layer to absorb the sweat before it cooled on my chest. (The science of it still sounds vague to me.) Anything is worth trying once. I was bought a set of singlets and told to wear them.

Rapidly, the boys in my class found out and my singlets came in for some withering mockery. We were twelve or thirteen at the time, and so, without surprise, the most frequent jape involved comparing the singlet to a bra, which the girls around us were just beginning to wear. After about a week of this, I resorted to the only act of sartorial rebellion I have ever committed. Every morning, upon getting off the bus at school, I would proceed to the boys' room, where in a cubicle I would shuck my singlet and bury it within my bag. Every afternoon, as soon as I returned home, I slipped the singlet on again when I changed out of my uniform.

This became a wholly unexceptional habit of my school day. As far as my parents were concerned, I was diligently protecting my chest; as far as my classmates were concerned, I had stopped wearing my boy-bra. When it became clear, after several months, that the presumptive treatment-via-singlet wasn't fending off my chest congestions the way it was supposed to, the idea was dropped altogether. I never wore one again; in fact, when I shifted schools in the ninth grade, after we moved to Madras, I suddenly became the only boy in my class who *didn't* have a banyan on under his shirt.

Our uniform in Madras was the simplest of the three: a white, half-sleeved shirt; white or blue canvas shoes; blue shorts that turned, in our final years of school, into blue trousers. (I welcomed the trousers so much—as cover for my legs, spindliest of all the boys' in my class—that I continue to favour pants over shorts to this day.) In this school, there was no fussing about with seasonal sub-routines; there was no distinction between regular clothes and PT clothes. I was thrilled. Without knowing it, I think, I sublimated that simplicity into a platonic model of how to dress. Some of my friends from the same Madras school are even further along the spectrum than I am, to the point that we might be accused of upside-down vanity—an inattention to appearance that is as scrupulous and conscientious as an attention to appearance. All our wardrobes, I'll wager, bear some manifest hallmarks: sober colours; lots of jeans; cotton shirts that are either plain or checked; clothes that are worn for years and years, as long as they continue to fit and aren't conspicuously frayed. To the dismay of the women in my family, I still wear some shirts—out in public!—that I bought eighteen years ago, when I set out for college.

The uniform prescribed by our Madras school resembled something a production-line worker might wear at a factory, and that analogy was, in a way, appropriate. Like so many other high schools around India, this was a hub of industrial-strength cramming: memorizing volumes of information, so that you might do well in your fortnightly tests, which would enable you to do well in your term-end exams, which would enable you to do well in your finals. We were at school from 8.15 a.m. to 2.45 p.m., with a twenty-minute break for lunch; then we went home, spent the late afternoon doing homework, and, on several evenings a week, attended supplementary tuitions. The weekends were for extended homework sets; holidays were consumed with homework. The school—to be fair, the education system—denied the concept of any sort of rest or respite for pupils. If we wanted to do anything else, we had to hack the time for it out of our days, like an inexperienced surgeon forced to extract an organ from a patient with the help of just a sharp rock.

I struggle, then, to work out why I was so happy during those years—or why, to be more precise, I regard those years, in retrospect, as among the happiest of my life. My tentative conclusion, at least until I reach a new one, is that I associate happiness with a requirement to have to make as few decisions as possible. Our matrix of decision-making explodes the moment school ends and it seems to keep growing through the better part of adulthood—a ramifying symphony of minor and major judgements to make, factors to consider, things to worry about. Whom to meet, where to stay, what to do next Friday night, how to deal with love and death and taxes. These questions and a million others are the very stuff of human existence; we live only by trying to answer them. But it strikes me, frequently, that we expend our days in the process—that we are so besieged by these questions that we are unable to devote ourselves to the one or two or three things we care most truly about. It sounds incredible, but what I seem to cherish in those final four years of school was the inability to control my own life. The big and middling decisions were being made elsewhere, by others; only one thing was required of me—that I perform creditably at my studies. This state of affairs was, paradoxically, liberating: it released me to enjoy the smaller weave of my life. Like a Mondrian painting, my childhood had clean lines, and I miss them.

How dangerous and unwelcome this preference would be in its political parallel, I realize. It would spiral quickly into tyranny, in which citizens are content to give up their independence and the state seizes their powers. I'm unable to square this difference between the ideal mechanisms for the lived life versus the political life. But as children, we knew no other way to be except in a condition of what the Stoics called *amor fati*—a love of fate; that, it turns out, may be the most sensible way for us to live. 'Do not seek to have everything that happens happen as you wish,' the

Stoic philosopher Epictetus, who spent his youth as a slave, wrote, 'but wish for everything to happen as it actually does happen, and your life will be serene.'

My *amor fati* has mostly crumbled since I left school, but one filament of it has somehow survived in the clothes I possess. They have imported forward all the principles of the school uniform. Everyone is, really, equal. Clothes don't make the man. A pair of dark blue trousers is magnificent in its own way. Forgetting what people are wearing can be a virtue. To relinquish control, in many circumstances, is the greatest blessing of all.

What She Left Behind

Kyung-Sook Shin

Translated from the Korean by
Young-Lahn Chung

I once heard that there is an observatory at Gimpo Airport where you could watch planes take off.

Someone told me that he visited the observatory whenever he felt as though his body and soul were filled with some indescribable thing beyond his control. Gazing at planes soaring from the ground for one or two hours, or sometimes for half a day, he said, cleared his troubled mind of hatred towards others, self-directed pessimism and anxiety towards the past, present and future.

*

I have not visited the observatory myself, but upon first hearing of it, I was reminded of a friend who I had met through work, a long time ago. At the time, I was an aspiring writer and had yet to write my first book. I was making a living as a scriptwriter for a classical music radio programme, which afforded me a generous amount of free time. My job was to write a number of lines for the host to narrate between musical pieces during a two-hour radio show. Each morning at dawn, I would seclude myself in the writers' room at the radio station to write scripts for two hours, and then return to my own little apartment. In fact, I had chosen this job as a last resort with the aim to become a writer, since I could work a few hours in the morning and then spend the rest of the day writing my own manuscript. Most of the time, the writers' room was empty in the hours when I was there. The silence there offered the perfect quietude for me to focus on work. When the morning broke and other scriptwriters began to crowd the room, I placed my finished work on the producer's desk and returned home while watching commuters travel to work.

Then one day, a woman began to appear at the writers' room around the same time as I did. I do not recall the radio show whose scripts she wrote. But as she entered a space that was once empty and hollow, her presence somehow lent me a sense of relief. At dawn, the radio station building always looked desolate, even grotesque and when I got on the elevator and hit the button for the fifth floor, the shrill chime resonated with a deafening volume in my ears. As I navigated through the long, deserted hallway alone, an unfathomable tension began to well up inside, which compelled me to look behind over my shoulders. Then, one day, I began to find that the light in the writers' room was already on and she would be there before me, writing her scripts. She had exorcized the bizarre tension that I had previously felt upon walking into the writers' room alone.

Less than a month after meeting her, I discovered a few things about her.

Out of all the women that I knew at the time, she was the first to obtain a driver's licence. She wore the heaviest make-up, changed her hairstyle most frequently and had the smallest hands. And the detail that baffled me most was that she owned the most clothes among my female friends. Not a single day would pass by when she wore the same outfit as the day before, despite coming to work at such an early hour. I also noticed that her wardrobe essentially had no fixed colour palette or style. A wildly coloured jacket, which most girls would not even try on, suited her perfectly. One day, she would wear a dress and on another, a blouse and a skirt. I tried to count the different jackets that she wore, and promptly gave up.

By then, it is likely that she also realized several things about me.

I was unique to her as she was to me, in the sense that I was the one among all the girls she knew who wore the least make-up, had the least number of clothes, most stubbornly insisted on keeping the same hairstyle and probably had the biggest hands.

These two opposite people sat opposite each other in the writers' room and wrote in the early hours of the morning almost every day. In the meantime, a friendship began to grow. She was the only person I talked to during this period of my life, and the vice versa was likewise true for her.

We were paid by the number of scripts we wrote, as opposed to a fixed monthly salary. Although the writer's fee for each day was modest, thirty days' worth of payments in one lot amounted to a considerable sum. Once she was paid, she went shopping for clothes without fail. She never seemed to get tired of buying more clothes. Thanks to her, I came to know that you could find uniquely designed clothes at Bangsan Market near Dongdaemun Market. I also learned that you could buy American or Indian clothes at stores down certain alleys in Itaewon, without having to travel to those faraway countries. I occasionally accompanied her in wandering around such clothes stores in the labyrinthine maze of Bangsan Market and Itaewon. You could buy a bolt of fabric at Dongdaemun Market and have it tailored into a dress at a shop in Itaewon. It seems that, every once in a while, youth is an opportunity to deeply indulge in something that may seem entirely irrelevant.

I had little interest in clothes at the time, but it felt as though I visited almost every dress shop in Seoul. I never bought an item of clothing for myself, but I spent countless hours beside her as she shopped. And just the same, she never bought any books, but she accompanied me as I browsed through shelves and bought books. Holding her hand tightly lest I lost her in the maze of Bangsan Market, I watched her as she shopped for clothes. I still remember that my palm would become slippery with sweat as I held her delicate hand. Once, we visited an old bookstore that I had frequented for a long time for its big closing-down sale. As I was hunched over piles of books to pick up one more book, she waited for me, while quietly adjusting her clothes. It was not only inexpensive clothes from local shops at Bangsan Market that she bought. At times, she bought expensive, brand-name clothes that cost more than her monthly payment. Her bank account was constantly overdrawn. I began to worry about her and one day, I asked her, 'Why are you buying more clothes when you already have so many?'

Instead of replying, she simply tilted her head and asked me her own question.

'Why do you buy another book when you already have so many?'

Lost for words by her unexpected question, I could only meekly stare back into her eyes.

'You buy books, I buy clothes. The only difference is that my clothes cost more money,' she continued.

How can you say that those two are the same? I wanted to retort. But I decided to keep my silence, knowing that her next question would ask how they were different. Back then, my tiny rented room was overflowing with books, amidst which I had made a small clearing to curl up and sleep. There was no more space to store books in my room, but still I couldn't help but buy a few more. I frequented bookstores as though I had a hunger for reading. And each time, I came out with a bundle of books in my hands. I even came to sleep with my head resting on books, instead of a pillow. I could not advise her to stop buying clothes even though I knew that her habit had resulted in debt. Because I worried that she would also insist that I stop buying books.

Dressed in her fancy clothes, she would occasionally visit Gimpo Airport. It was much before the opening of Incheon International Airport. When she told me she had been to the airport, at first I wondered whether she had some kind of appointment there. However, she visited the airport quite often. So, one day when she told me that she had been to the airport again, I asked her, 'Why do you go there so often?'

She did not reply.

'Do you have a friend who is a flight attendant?'

'No.'

'Do you have any friends living there?'

'No.'

'Then why do you go there?'

It seemed that she herself had never thought about the reason she went to the airport so often.

As I asked her again, she answered, 'Just because.'

'Just because?'

'Yes!'

'You mean you dress yourself up to go to the airport for no particular reason?'

'I'm just happy to watch people boarding planes at the airport,' she said.

I stared at her blankly. I thought we had become friends by the time, but suddenly she was a stranger to me. She said she had got her driver's licence just so she could drive to the airport in her fancy clothes. Gimpo Airport was the first destination that she drove to upon obtaining her licence and completing the driving practice.

Whether in personal relationships or in professional settings, there are times when you have to make the first move to depart. Between her and me, I quit the scriptwriting job first. On my last day at the writers' room, she gifted me a jacket. It was a brown jacket of an expensive brand that I had never worn before. The reason why I still call her my friend actually owes to the significance of this jacket. For her, giving away her own clothes was a sign of sincere friendship. I knew that she took meticulous care of her clothes, with no exceptions. The jacket that she gave me was the most expensive and finest outfit in my entire collection. Unfortunately, it did not suit me very well, but I hung this precious gift from the best spot in my closet for years. When I turned thirty, a friend was travelling to Germany to study abroad and I gave her the brown jacket. She wore the jacket on her flight leaving Seoul.

Years passed by without contact between my scriptwriter friend and me. Then one day, more than a decade later, she called me on the telephone. Even before I could ask who was calling, I recognized her voice and instantly recalled the countless outfits that she used to wear at work. Soon after, one summer day during the rainy season, we met for lunch at a restaurant in Insa-dong. She hadn't changed a bit. She was wearing fancy clothes and still worked at the broadcasting station. She now seemed to regularly visit the newly built Incheon International Airport, instead of Gimpo Airport. 'So, you must have travelled a lot by now?' I asked her. But she replied that she had not. She had still never flown in a plane. Once again, she appeared to become a person that I barely knew and I could only stare at her again. As if she suddenly recalled something, she asked me, 'You still buy lots of books, right?'

'Yeah ... I suppose.'

'I bought the book that you wrote. And that was my first time spending money on something other than clothes,' she said.

People seldom change. Realizing that neither of us had changed whatsoever, I burst into a fit of laughter. The sound of the falling rain dashed in between us from time to time. About another ten years after our lunch together, I heard from a producer at the radio station that my friend had passed away. One winter morning, she was found collapsed on the floor of the elevator on her way in to work. She was wearing a fine winter coat and a scarf around her neck. In the desolate early hours, the elevator lingered on the fifth floor until her lifeless body was found.

Even when I was not in touch with her, I thought about her whenever I saw elegant clothes. Perhaps she had thought about me whenever she saw books.

*

I often fly for business trips and private trips. Every time I go to the airport to board a flight, I am reminded of her. I wonder if she is somewhere at the airport in her fine clothes, watching my plane take off from the runway. Sometimes I find myself looking around. Why did she spend time and money to dress up and drive all the way to the airport, only to watch the planes taking off? Why didn't she get on a plane herself? What was on her mind as she watched each plane take to the air? Did she put on her fancy clothes and visit the airport to clear her troubled mind of hatred towards others, self-directed pessimism and anxiety towards the past, present and future?

I may never know.

THE OXFORD DRESS

PLUM SYKES

There is one dress in my life that seems to sum up everything I dreamed about when I was seventeen. It was the dress I wore to my Oxford University interview, in the winter of 1987.

When I received the news that I had been offered an interview for a possible place at Oxford, aside from going into severe panic mode about my knowledge of history, my chosen subject, I suffered a meltdown about what to wear. I was seventeen years old and had spent most of my teens dressed in an ugly brown school uniform during the school week, and in riding kit on the weekends. I had very few 'smart' clothes—the only dressy items I needed during my teens were black tie frocks for the occasional debutante parties I'd started going to.

So, I had an odd wardrobe consisting mainly of school wear, jodhpurs and about three 'ball gowns' as I rather grandly called them. The 'ball gowns' were actually party dresses that my mother, who was a fashion designer, had had made for me, or my grandmother whizzed up for me on her sewing machine. My favourite one was a strapless, dark purple silk taffeta dress that was long enough to almost reach my ankles. It had a gathered waist and was a very

1980s look—the kind of thing that young, slightly Sloane-y girls would wear to dance all night at weekend parties. I also adored the 'puffball' dress that Granny had sewn for me. This was a slightly more fashion forward frock: inspired by the faintly ridiculous Christian Lacroix dresses that were on all the runways at the time, mine was made of red and white striped silk crepe de Chine. It had a strapless, corseted bodice with a mini skirt attached that was stuffed with net to make it puff out. I thought I looked absolutely marvellous in it, but, in reality I looked like an upside-down mushroom.

You can see why I had nothing to wear for my Oxford interview. I didn't have any money to go and buy clothes. But I desperately wanted to look immaculate.

My main resource was my mother and her team of seamstresses. In that fall of 1987, I remember leafing through endless copies of British *Vogue* in search of inspiration. I knew that I wanted to wear a dress, but I didn't want anything too girly or frou-frou. For some reason—and this has been a lifelong theme in my wardrobe—I have never felt particularly strong or confident in floaty, floppy clothes. Although I'm not someone who, at that stage in my life, had worn a great deal of tailoring, I knew that a strong silhouette made me feel good. My main experience of a well-cut jacket was the heavenly riding coat passed down from my grandmother—even then I knew that a beautiful line, whether on horseback or on foot, could give aesthetic and spiritual backbone.

One evening after school, when I was yet again leafing through the latest copy of British *Vogue*, I came across a photograph of Christy Turlington dressed in a double-breasted, navy blue, velvet coat dress. It had a large sailor-style collar in pale pink satin and eight large pale pink buttons running down the front. It was very short—I don't think it came much below Christy's thighs—but it was neatly tailored, sharp. I suppose the look was 1980s power dressing for young girls. I seized on this as the ideal interview outfit if only it could be a few inches longer.

My mother, Valerie, was completely open to the idea of designing the pattern for the coat dress and set to work on it immediately. When I look back now, I am in awe of the fact that my mum could, seemingly so effortlessly, produce an incredible piece of tailoring for her daughter in a short space of time with absolutely no sense of stress. (To my utter shame I have to admit that I have only ever sewed one skirt for my daughter Ursula. It took an entire day and tried my patience sorely.) Mum's skill was—and still is—cutting beautiful patterns. She did this for the coat dress. I chose a navy blue wool and then she cut it out and sent it off to her most skilled sample machinist. It was returned a week or so later, and I tried it on. It fit perfectly on my rather giraffe-like proportions, with a narrow silhouette and sharp shoulders. The skirt was a little longer than the version Christy wore in *Vogue*—it hit me just above the knee—and the sleeves were sleek and narrow. I had honestly never looked as well dressed in my life.

The day of my Oxford interview soon arrived. I remember being thoroughly intimidated when I arrived at Worcester

College one freezing December morning. The college has an imposing gatehouse which opens into a magnificent quadrangle with a huge lawn and imposing Georgian buildings—it looked more like a mini country estate than an educational establishment.

I soon found myself in the Porter's Lodge with a few other interviewees. We were given keys to various rooms (we all had to stay two nights) and a list of interview times. My interview was not until the following day so I had a lot of time to kill before then. I spent the day revising, feeling extremely nervous.

That night, all the interviewees had dinner in the grand dining room in college. It was a lovely room, painted a beautiful pale blue with stunning plaster swags and cornicing on the walls and ceiling. The food was atrocious, but I remember thinking what a wonderful place to have supper—and how dreamy it would be if I were to get into this remarkable university. After supper, a rather good-looking public school boy came up to me and invited me out for a drink. I was terribly excited. I'd never been asked on a date. We went to a scruffy local pub. It wasn't in the least bit romantic and I remember feeling very, very disappointed by my first 'date'.

The next morning, I got up very, very early in a state of high anticipation about my interview. I buttoned myself into the wonderful navy blue coat dress, added black opaque tights and mid-heeled suede pumps. My long, honey-brown hair reached almost to my elbows and I brushed it out so that it swirled around my shoulders. I put on a tiny dash of mascara and lip gloss—that was all I needed at the age of seventeen.

All the interviewees met for an early breakfast in the dining hall. I soon realized that I was overdressed compared with most of the other students. No one else was wearing a tailor-made dress. Most of them were boys and I recall them wearing bland trousers and jackets. The food on offer was spectacularly basic—white toast with Marmite, cereal, or greasy eggs and bacon. I was too anxious to eat very much but I managed to gulp down some tea and a few spoons of cornflakes.

My interview was scheduled for around ten in the morning. I will never forget clambering up the steep staircase to the rooms of a don named Mr Harry Pitt. The staircase was painted black below the dado rail, plain cream above, and as a result, seemed cold and poky. I was very glad with my dress: not only was it wonderful looking, it was made of wool and encased me in warmth. I knocked on Pitt's door and was soon summoned.

I was met by a quintessentially Oxford scene. Harry Pitt, a diminutive man in his sixties, was the Modern History don. He was dressed in a dark suit and tie and was wearing thick, Clark Kent-style glasses. His brown hair was brushed over to one side, in a rather old-fashioned, 1950s way. He shook my hand and gestured for me to sit down on a worn sofa. I did so and soon noticed, to my surprise, that there appeared to be a body snoozing on the chaise longue opposite.

'That's Professor Campbell,' Mr Pitt told me, unfazed.

Suddenly the body on the sofa grunted. There was a lot of harrumphing and grumbling and the Professor hauled himself up, bid me hello and promptly lay back down again. Meanwhile, Mr Pitt lit his pipe, inhaled deeply, shut his eyes and soon started bombarding me with historical questions.

As far as I could tell, neither don had taken the least bit of notice of my dress–quite rightly.

I don't recall very much about the interview apart from fact that I fretted about my answers. The only question I remember clearly was when Harry Pitt asked me why did I think that Adolf Hitler was able to be such a sensitive painter as well as being a mass murderer. Whenever anyone asks me what kind of questions one gets asked in an Oxford interview, I always tell them about that Hitler question. 'What did you say?' they ask. They are crestfallen when I tell them with complete honesty that I cannot remember even one word of my answer.

The rest of the day was spent skulking around and looking at the noticeboard in the Porter's Lodge every few hours–this was where news of any more interviews would be posted.

The format for Oxford interviews is confusing: if they pass the 'Oxbridge' entrance exam, potential students are offered an interview at the college of their first choice, as I had been (Oxford University is made up of thirty-three colleges). If the college wants to offer the student a place, the student is not told this immediately, but is not offered an interview at their second choice of college. If the college doesn't want to offer a student place, but they don't believe that the student will get into the second choice college, this also means that they are not offered an interview at their second choice college. If the college doesn't want to offer the student a place but does think that they deserve a place at Oxford University, they send them to the second choice of college for an interview. However, just to confuse things, being sent to a second interview does not necessarily mean that your first choice of college doesn't want you—sometimes it means that the first choice college may want you but isn't sure yet.

The outcome all interviewees are looking for after their first interview is not to be sent on to their second choice of college in the hope that this is because they have secured a place at their first choice of college. But, equally, they know that not being sent on to a second interview could be a sign that they didn't get in to their first choice of college and that there is no chance of a place at the second choice either. So, either way, whether an interviewee gets another interview or doesn't, they are none the wiser about their possible chances.

It turned out that no news at all was posted that day on the noticeboard. So, there we were, a bunch of anxiety-ridden teenagers who all had to stay a second night in Oxford awaiting some kind of news the next day.

It turned out that I was not offered a second interview at another college. My self-confidence and my intellectual self-esteem were not high when I was that age. I was convinced that I had not got in, and soon departed the beautiful town to go back to my school in another part of England.

A few weeks later, the Christmas holidays started. The coat dress was back in my closet and I had put the Oxford application to the back of my mind as something very exciting happened. My twin sister Lucy and I were invited by Anna Wintour, who was then the editor of American *House & Garden*, to go to New York for two nights to be photographed for her magazine. We had never travelled outside Europe. It was dizzying to be in America, in New York City for the first time, with all the razzmatazz that surrounded a fashion shoot.

I think we had been in New York for one night when, very early the next morning, the phone rang in the hotel room. It was my mother. She said that she was ringing to tell me that the reply had come from Oxford. Even though it was addressed to me she had not been able to stop herself from opening it.

'You got in!' she shrieked.

I'll never forget that navy blue coat dress.

A Dress is Like a Field

TISHANI DOSHI

A dress is like a field. Lift a hem and flowers
will fall. Fold it in a wooden chest and weeds
will lay their fingers against its cotton heart.
A dress is sin. Take Marilyn. Take subway grate.
Take *you must have had to paint that on you.*
Flamenco ruffle, zipper, Cleopatra in gold lamé.
Little. Black. Something. When we were girls,
we played at dressing up—mum's swimsuit
with built-in bosoms, a lesson in seduction.
The past is a yard in Wales. My mother
and her sister in matching seersucker frocks,
hands in pockets, high collars, the wind
making petticoats of their hair. They join
a ship of sisters. Mothers with needles
and thread, holding bolts of cloth against
their chests, thinking, this will do, this will sail
them across the years. A Singer sewing machine
in Madras. My sister and I in handmade smocks
with floral bibs and frills. Aspiring Zazous with high
socks and lacunae of knees. If I had daughters
I'd dress them in velvet suits with cummerbunds,
and they would long to roll down meadows,

to scorch the wilds of their insides against grass.
A dress needs only a mosquito net to be a bride,
and later, as it yellows in a bag, it will dream
of being a factory girl, a school child, something lumpen
and uniform, to recognize itself in the other.
A dress never loses its sense of the dramatic.
It knows how to languish across a washing line,
how to beckon from a mannequin, how to sit
puddled on a floor. See this riverbank–
there's a row of them, unbelted, unbuttoned.
The river calls for skin, the dress shrugs off like winter.
An afternoon of love, a picnic, clots of copper maple.
Legs of bone, seams turned towards the sun. Nothing
like abandoned shoes, which glow with horror,
the piles at Dachau, trains, gunshots, dead bodies in water.
A dress is a forest of memory. Its damask skin,
its armpits of toil and wonder. Even the holes
are altars to fairy tales, reminding you how once
you were so small. Once your waist was a secret nation.

A PRINCE'S KAFTAN

KANISHK THAROOR

The prince of Portugal was not princely; he was not young, not dashing, not, strictly speaking, an heir (the king of Portugal, after all, was his nephew), not particularly foolish either since he had already made his most calamitous mistakes, nor was he amorous—even if he willed it, the flesh was weak. Centuries later, in the light of their own overseas conquests, the British called him Henry the Navigator. They imagined him as a kind of forebear, even though he had no children and never had a wife. In his own time, he was known as the Duke of Viseu or, more often, as the Infant. It was a title he held as a baby, but also as a boy and then as a teenaged crusader, as an avowed bachelor, as a jowly merchant lord and slave-trader, and now as the old man who seethed alone in his bed at the dullness of the dawn, debating whether to play dress-up with the robe of the Sultan.

He laid waiting for his servant Alvisu to come into the room and draw the curtains. At that point, he would make a great show of blinking and yawning, as if the light had just woken him. Robust men know how to sleep, the Infant believed, but wakefulness was the mark of an uneasy mind. There was no sign of Alvisu, nor any sound in the hallway of the manor rousing itself. He tried to tell what time it was from the thickness of the light falling beneath the drapes. At this hour, the bakers should have already stuffed the ovens full of loaves. Boys would be groggily tending to the horses in the stables. His secretaries would be getting shaved and brushing the lint from their hats. *Where is Alvisu?* he thought, yearning for his foot-rub. Perhaps it was even earlier than he assumed. There was enough light warming the darkness of his room that he could make out the canopy of his bed and the small black shapes of flies jumping over the mesh. *I'm getting old*, he thought, *I'm getting too old for mornings.*

Impatient, he did what he hated doing by himself. He got out of bed. Without Alvisu's help, the process was more of an ordeal. He found it difficult to tip-toe as he would have done in previous years, to protect himself from the sudden irredeemable cold of the floor. As usual, his slippers had scuttled under the bed on their own. The Infant pondered for a moment if it was worth it, if a man of his age and station in life really had to endure the indignity of bending. But then he imagined Alvisu coming into the room and finding his master dishevelled and barefoot. Slowly, like the winching down of a foundation stone, the Infant lowered himself to his knees and retrieved his slippers. It didn't matter to him that the red silk was frayed beyond repair, that the nails of his big toes had poked holes in the felt lining. After a decade of morning ablutions wearing these slippers, he felt that he belonged to them as much as they belonged to him.

In the old Moorish style, his room faced an internal

courtyard. The curtains were far too heavy for him in his enfeebled seniority to pull aside, so he batted his way to the parting and looked out the window. It was early still, the light seeping blue from a distant dawn. A slave-woman with a hand broom swept the stone paving, holding her bonnet in place as she progressed like an earthworm from one end to the other, brushing clean a floor that would in a few hours be splashed with mud and horse shit. She drew a bucket from the central well and scattered the water liberally across the stone to damp down the dust. Everybody knew dust made the Infant grumpy and his eyes water. She began sweeping again. Watching her, he heard the scraping of her broom in the base of his throat, where it gathered in tingling strength and lifted through his passageways in a clarifying sneeze. The woman looked up from her work and for a moment held the gaze of the old man in the window, his wet eyes and red nose, her panting mouth, before both slave and master gasped at the recognition of the other. She lowered her face and the Infant retreated through the curtains into the dark of his bedroom.

It was September and old men—he was a great uncle many times over—are allowed to feel the chill even then. Stubbornly, he had refused to let the fireplace be lit. He pinched the logs that had been stacked there uselessly through the summer. They were damp. *Alvisu will have to make my grog the English way today*, the Infant thought, *and before I do anything else, I'll soak my feet in hot water and salts.* He sat on the edge of the bed, his slippers dangling from his feet. *Perhaps I should go back to sleep*, he thought. But the dim sight of the rumpled sheet and pillows filled him with an almost physical terror.

He felt his way towards a cupboard to look for a shawl. Evidently, he did not know where the shawls were kept. He found stack after stack of boots. The circle of royal sovereignty can be very wide, even when its circle of intimate knowledge is rather narrow. In the softening dark, he bumped around the corner to a dismal place, his personal wardrobe.

Whenever the servants allowed him a glimpse inside, the Infant's wardrobe appeared like nightfall over the sea, the interminable sheets of black, the timid intrusion of some blue. Every day was a succession of brooding doublets and wide-brimmed hats, getting darker all the time, as if he were being dressed for the grave. He had been complaining to his attendants. *Give me some red, for God's sake, some orange, a touch of the sun.* They bowed as they knew well to but deferred to Alvisu, who would veto the Infant's request. *This is your plan*, Alvisu would remind his master, *to dress as befits your esteemed station, as a wise counsellor to the king.* Like most leaders, the Infant bristled when his ideas were repeated back to him. Each time he caught a glance of his reflection, he bared his teeth and hissed at the gloomy spectre of himself.

Decades ago, so far back it felt to the Infant like a remote biblical epoch, he was famous for the way he dressed. In his private court, he would celebrate the feast days of the great saints with a shimmer of silks, brightly coloured tunics, belts with ornate clasps, cloaks lined with the silvering fur of creatures the Infant could hardly imagine. Tailors, milliners, and cordwainers from as far afield as Burgundy and Genoa supplied him with the latest fashions of the northern courts, the priciest fabrics of the east. For the feast of St Anthony, he once arrayed the young noblemen who kept him company in streams of taffeta and they bustled about the hall like a flock of tropical birds. Nobody in Portugal could match the Infant's gallants for spectacle, for the bravery of their dress.

Now, his young retainers were no longer young. They spent their days in the hall spitting bones into the rushes, hankering after the maids and slaves. Their boredom reminded the Infant of his own diminishing. He was too old to hunt, so that obvious pastime of male companions could not be offered to the few noblemen left to him. His great debts required him to be pious and to avoid the excess of jousts and martial games. And as a prince ennobled by austerity, the Infant could not allow his men to appear in public in colours other than black, grey and blue. Only through this very visible sobriety, Alvisu often reminded him, would the Infant earn a return to the good graces of the king, or win back the trust of the parliament. The prince sighed. It agonized him that he lived in a self-serious age when even the little shock of white was considered brazen.

But was it wrong for an old man to be brazen in private? The Infant stubbed his toe against a familiar chest. Swearing, he knelt to open it. Dust sneezed from the creaking lid. After removing layers of protective paper, he lifted out a Turkish kaftan. Mothballs rained from its creases. It was the garment that he liked to call the robe of the Sultan, though he had no idea who wore it and who it was meant for. Years ago, his privateers stormed a Muslim merchant's ship in the Mediterranean and gifted a portion of the loot to the Infant, including this otherworldly robe. Bending a bit under its weight, he brought it towards the light of the window.

At first, it seemed to shine. The Infant marvelled at its whiteness, purer than milk, a colour summoned down from a spring cloud. He let his fingers brush over the embroidered rivers of gold that flamed up the sleeves. The high collar was burnished with silk that limned the seams and hems. For a long moment, the Infant caressed the kaftan's folds, pressing his nose to the velvet as if he were meeting an old friend or nuzzling a lover.

The Infant spread his arms wide and let the kaftan enfold him. Were the usual guards, chambermaids and attendants around, they would have noticed the Infant grow indisputably taller. The glow of the robe suffused his face and lifted him above the earth. He floated. His threadbare slippers made no sound on the stone. He imagined himself as a dove, flapping his arms slowly. Then he spun and watched the ribbed skirts of the kaftan follow him in a delicate wave. Nobody saw him at play in the Sultan's robe, nobody except for Alvisu, who the Infant knew more as a shadow than a person, who watched his master quietly from the doorway, debating the right moment to step in and interrupt the lonely pageant.

Not just yet. The Infant had made himself dizzy and lost one slipper. He steadied himself on the post of the bed and smiled. The alien fabric caused the hairs of his arms stand on end, a secret thrill shivering down his spine. He enjoyed wearing the robe with nobody around. It was his way, he had convinced himself, of better understanding the infidel enemy, that foe whose utter defeat was and would always be the object of his life.

The Infant turned his back on his private shrine with its portraits of saints and its replica cross, its occasional incense, its heaps of rosaries refreshed with the blessings of both Portuguese and Spanish bishops. Then he took a cloth and wrapped his head in a manner of turban and imagined he was an emir or a bey or even a sultan. *For Mahomet*, he intoned, *for Illahi*. Inevitably, he thought of Morocco and the seawalls of Ceuta, of sitting on a horse or a camel at the head of a swarm of riders, their black and green flags rippling above the dusty fray, or of the weight of a scimitar held aloft, its blade burnished with spiralling incantations to a preposterous God, or of the black-rimmed eyes and thick eyebrows of the concubines in the harem. He sat on the foot of the bed with his eyes shut, willing himself into the mind of an infidel lord.

But it was morning, he was hungry and he found his thoughts drifting elsewhere, to matters more mundane. What's best worn underneath the robe? Maybe nothing at all? Could it be that the sultans are entirely naked under their finery? He thought of the Atlantic winds chasing up his bare calves, and clutched the robe closer to his body. How long did it take the heathens to make such a beautiful piece of clothing? Were there ateliers specially meant for the production of fine robes for nobles? Or could it be, he wondered, that not just the powerful men of those places wear nice clothes, but the traders and labourers, too, and maybe, who knows, even the slaves? It would be damning for Portugal and all Christendom if slaves over there dressed better than princes over here. *That's impossible*, he thought, brushing the flowing fabric, the cascade of white and gold. Nobody, not even the Mahometans, would waste this on a slave.

In these moments, an odd feeling would sometimes overwhelm the Infant, a dismaying sense of his tiny share of the earth. More than other Christian princes and kings—and certainly more than his brothers and their jabbering sons—the Infant was famous for his worldliness. It was at his behest, after all, that ships bearing white, God-fearing men had sailed south and east, unravelling the bounds of Africa and discovering strange, remote islands deep in the ocean. Under his direction, Portugal's little markets had become emporiums, filled with all manner of products, from fantastic molluscs to sugar cane to the fine wood of Madeira to the blackest slaves. Both the Jewish mapmakers of Majorca and monkish Italian cartographers would pester his ship captains for their logs, for the latest inventories of coastlines and harbours. It was through his will that tiny Portugal on the margins of Europe could claim some measure of larger standing.

And yet often when he wore this foreign robe, the world would recede from him. The garment hid more than it revealed. There was a whole mysterious civilization for whom this robe held all sorts of obvious meanings and was, if not commonplace, at least not exotic. But it remained in some sense unfathomable to the Infant. He imagined a sultan—aquiline nose, dignified beard, the watery eyes of the entitled—pondering the daily garb of a Portuguese prince, the hose and breeches, the swelling doublets, the floundering hat, all of it at once impractical and severe. The Muslim would be amused, of course, at the ridiculous assemblage. In the seeming solitude of his room, the Infant heard, first in the back of his head and then ringing around his skull, the laughter of men he would never know.

Gasping, he ripped off the linen turban and stumbled to his feet. He struggled with the pegs and buttons of the robe, trying to throw it off. *Let me help you, lord,* Alvisu said and finally made himself known. *Get me out of this thing,* the Infant barked. Alvisu snapped his fingers and further attendants streamed in from the hallway. They relieved the Infant of the robe of the Sultan, carrying it arm to arm to the wardrobe as if they were supporting a drunk. His servant came close. *I thought you might like your grog the English way,* Alvisu said, *it's a cold morning.*

The Infant nodded and held the warm mug to his chin. The curtains were pulled aside and light, like fresh air, flooded into the room. In his linen shift and with one slipper on, he walked over to the window. The steam from the fortified wine fogged the glass. Outside, the slave had her back to him as she finished her sweeping. The Infant could now make out the furled sails and masts of a few ships in the harbour and then the cold grey line of the sea, which once seemed to him like an open invitation, but was now altogether more implacable, a reminder of his shrinking horizons.

Alvisu cleared his throat to speak, but the Infant cut him short. *Cancel the morning correspondence*, the prince said. *I'm going to go back to bed.*

The Exchange

JHUMPA LAHIRI

TRANSLATED FROM THE ITALIAN BY
ANN GOLDSTEIN

There was a woman, a translator, who wanted to be another person. There was no precise reason. It had always been that way.

She had friends, a family, an apartment, a job. She had enough money, and good health. She had, in other words, a fortunate life, for which she was grateful. The only thing that troubled her was what distinguished her from others.

When she thought of what she possessed, she felt a mild revulsion, because every object, every thing that belonged to her, gave proof of her existence. Every time she remembered something of her past life, she was convinced that another version would have been better.

She considered herself imperfect, like the first draft of a book. She wanted to produce another version of herself, in the same way that she could transform a text from one language into another. At times she had the impulse to remove her presence from the earth, as if it were a thread on the hem of a nice dress, to be cut off with a pair of scissors.

And yet she didn't want to kill herself. She loved the world too much, and people. She loved taking long walks in the late afternoon and observing her surroundings. She loved the green of the sea, the light of dusk, the rocks scattered on the sand. She loved the taste of a red pear in autumn, the full, heavy winter moon that shone amid the clouds. She loved the warmth of her bed, a good book to read without being interrupted. To enjoy that, she would have lived forever.

Wishing to better understand the reason she felt the way she did, she decided one day to eliminate the signs of her existence. Apart from a small suitcase, she threw or gave everything away. She wanted to live in solitude, like a monk, in order to confront what she couldn't bear. To her friends, her family, the man who loved her, she said that she had to go away for a while.

She chose a city where she knew no one, didn't understand the language, where it wasn't too hot or too cold. She brought clothes that were as simple as possible, all black: a dress, a pair of shoes, and a soft, light wool sweater, with five small buttons.

She arrived as the season was changing. It was warm in the sun, cool in the shade. She rented a room. She walked for hours, wandered aimlessly, without speaking. The city was small, pleasant but without personality, without tourists. She heard the sounds, observed the people: some hurried to work, some sat on benches, like her, with a book or a cell phone, taking the sun. When she was hungry, she ate something sitting on a bench. When she was tired, she went to the movies.

The days grew short, dark. Gradually the trees lost their colours, their leaves. The translator's mind emptied. She began to feel light, anonymous. She imagined she was a falling leaf, like every other.

At night she slept well. In the morning she woke without worries. She didn't think of the future or of the traces of her life. She was suspended in time, like a person without a shadow. And yet she was alive, she felt more alive than ever.

One rainy, windy day, she took shelter under the cornice of a stone building. The rain poured down. She didn't have an umbrella, or even a hat. The rain beat on the sidewalk with an insistent, continuous sound. She thought of the water's eternal journey, falling from the clouds, penetrating the earth, filling the rivers, arriving, finally, at the sea.

The street was pocked with puddles, the façade of the building opposite was covered with illegible signs. The translator noticed various women going in and out. Occasionally one alone or a small group would arrive, press a bell, then enter. Curious, she decided to follow.

Beyond the entranceway she had to cross a courtyard, where the rain was confined, as if it were falling in a room without a ceiling. She stopped for a moment to look at the sky, even though she got wet. Farther on, there was a dark stairway, the steps slightly uneven, where some women were coming down, others going up.

On the landing stood a tall, thin woman, with a wrinkled yet still beautiful face. She had short fair hair and was dressed in black. The dress was transparent, without a precise shape, and with long, diaphanous sleeves, like wings. This woman welcomed the others, with open arms.

Come in, come in, there are a lot of things to see. Inside the apartment the translator left her purse in the hall, on a long table, as the others did.

At the end of the hall was a large living room. A row of black dresses hung on a clothes rack next to the wall.

The dresses were like soldiers, at attention, but inanimate. In another part of the room there were couches, lighted candles, a table loaded with fruit, cheese, a rich chocolate cake. In a corner was a tall mirror divided into three, in which you could look at yourself from different angles.

The owner of the apartment, who had designed the black clothes, was sitting on a sofa, smoking and chatting. She spoke the language of the place perfectly, but with a slight accent. She was a foreigner, like the translator.

Welcome. Please, have something to eat, look around, make yourself comfortable.

Some women were already undressed and were trying on clothes, asking the others for their opinions. They were a collection of arms, legs, hips, waists. Unceasing variations. They all seemed to know each other.

The translator took off her sweater, undressed. She began to try on all the garments in her size, one after the other, methodically, as if it were a task. There were pants, jackets, skirts, shirts, dresses. All black, made of soft light fabrics.

They are ideal for travelling, the owner said. They are comfortable, modern, versatile. You can wash them by hand in cold water. They don't wrinkle.

The other women agreed. They said that now they wore

only clothes designed by the owner. You could get them only by going to her house, only by private invitation. Only in this way, secret, hidden, festive.

The translator stood in front of the mirror. She studied her own image. But she was distracted by the presence of another woman behind the mirror, at the end of the hall. She was different from the others. She was working at a table, with an iron, a needle in her mouth. She had tired eyes, a sorrowful face.

The clothes were elegant, well made. Even though they suited her, the translator didn't like them. After trying the last thing she decided to leave. She didn't feel like herself in those clothes. She didn't want to acquire or accumulate anything more.

There were piles of clothes everywhere, on the floor, on the couches, on the chairs, like so many dark puddles. After rummaging awhile, she found hers. But her black sweater was missing. She had looked in all the piles but hadn't found it.

The room was almost empty. While the translator was looking for her sweater, most of the women had left. The owner was preparing a receipt for the next to last. Only the translator remained.

The owner looked at her, as if she had noticed her presence for the first time.

'And what did you decide on?'

'Nothing. I'm missing a sweater, my own.'

'What colour?'

'Black.'

'Oh, I'm sorry.'

The owner called to the woman behind the mirror. She asked her to pick the clothes up off the floor, put everything in order.

'This lady is missing a black sweater,' she said. 'I don't know you,' she continued. 'How did you find me?'

'I was outside. I followed the others. I didn't know what was inside.'

'You don't like the clothes?'

'I like them but I don't need them.'

'Where are you from?'

'I'm not from here.'

'I'm not, either. Are you hungry? Would you like some wine? Fruit?'

'No, thank you.'

'Excuse me.'

It was the woman who worked for the owner. She showed something, a garment, to the translator.

'Here,' said the owner. 'It was hidden, we found your sweater.'

The translator took it. But she knew immediately, without even putting it on, that it wasn't hers. It was another one, unfamiliar. The wool was coarser, the black less intense, and it was a different size. When she put it on, when she looked in the mirror, the mistake seemed obvious to her.

'This isn't mine.'

'What do you mean?'

'Mine is similar, but this isn't it. I don't recognize this sweater. It doesn't fit.'

'But it must be yours. The maid has put everything in order. There's nothing on the floor, nothing on the couches, look.'

The translator didn't want to take the other sweater. She felt antipathy towards it, revulsion. 'This isn't mine. Mine has disappeared.'

'What do you mean?'

'Maybe another woman took it without realizing it. Maybe there was an exchange. Maybe there were other clients who were wearing a sweater like this?'

'I don't remember. All right, I can check, wait.'

The owner sat down again on the couch. She lit a cigarette. Then she began to make a series of calls. She explained to one woman after another what had happened. She said a few words to each one.

The translator waited. She was convinced that one of them had taken her sweater and that the one left for her belonged to someone else.

The owner put down the phone. 'I'm sorry. I've asked everyone. No one was wearing a black sweater here today. Only you.'

'But this isn't mine.'

She was sure that it wasn't hers. At the same time she felt a tremendous, consuming uncertainty that cancelled out everything, that left her with nothing.

'Thank you for coming, goodbye,' said the owner. She said nothing more.

The translator felt disconcerted, empty. She had come to that city looking for another version of herself, a transfiguration. But she understood that her identity was insidious, a root that she would never be able to pull up, a prison in which she would be trapped.

In the hall she wanted to say goodbye to the woman who worked for the owner, behind the mirror, at a table. But she was no longer there.

The translator returned home, defeated. She was forced to wear the other sweater, because it was still raining. That night she fell asleep without eating, without dreaming.

The next day, when she woke, she saw a black sweater on a chair in the corner of the room. It was again familiar to her. She knew that it had always been hers and that her reaction the day before, the little scene she had made in front of the two other women, had been completely irrational, absurd.

And yet this sweater was no longer the same, no longer the one she'd been looking for. When she saw it, she no longer felt revulsion. In fact, when she put it on, she preferred it. She didn't want to find the one she had lost, she didn't miss it. Now, when she put it on, she, too, was another.

Frida's Dress

Molly Crabapple

It is nearly impossible to draw Frida Kahlo.

You're probably laughing at me now. *Of course, you can draw Frida Kahlo,* you say. *Lots of artists have drawn Frida Kahlo. She's everywhere.* Frida has been photographed, sketched, painted, sculpted, silkscreened, traced, and remixed. Stores hawk Frida T-shirts. YouTube brims with Frida make-up tutorials. Tumblr whiz-bang-pops with blinking Frida GIFs. Street artists stencil Frida's features onto walls in Kerala and Istanbul, Paris and New York. Her trademark style is simple enough to meet James St James's rule for nightlife stardom: one can never be truly famous until they are recognizable in stick figure form. Fuck stick figures; to recognize Frida a viewer needs only to see her monobrow, the single line that she drew blacker and bolder in each of her fifty-five self-portraits. Frida painted her own face so often it became a subject as exclusive to her as the traditional Mexican fashion she remixed into armour. Until her death at the age of forty-seven, Frida braced her back with medical corsets, twisted roses into her braids, and painted herself into the status of an icon.

Despite her beauty, her uniqueness and her ubiquity, I could barely draw Frida Kahlo for this article. All my attempts looked, at best, like Photoshop filters upon the work of The Master. Her numina is too strong. She's no one's muse, and no one's model. Try and paint Frida Kahlo, and one just ends up adding to her body of work.

'The way she wore clothing was her *art*,' fashion writers like to gush, perhaps because shopping is many socialites' nearest brush with creativity, but in Frida's case, it's hard to say anything else. Like so much good art, her sartorial style grew out of disaster. A streetcar bearing the teenage Frida smashed into a lorry; her pelvis was impaled on an iron pole. The crash that shattered Frida's back trapped her in a prison of painful medical interventions. While on her first long bed rest, Frida learned to paint. Later, she turned her plaster medical corsets into canvases. One bears a hammer and sickle—Frida was a committed communist—along with a foetus that represented the child she could not have. You can see why French surrealist André Breton called Frida's art 'a ribbon wrapped around a bomb.' She never denied pain. Instead, with her art, she looked it frankly in the eye, and said, *yeah, I see you, you ugly beast. You think you're all powerful, but you're just my raw material, same as my brushes. I'll polish you and paint you and make you serve me. You'll be my most beautiful weapon of all.*

Frida hid her crippled left leg beneath long Mexican skirts for the first time when she was twenty-three, at her wedding to the god king of Mexican muralists, Diego Rivera. The floor-length green dress and red fringed shawl—*rebazo*—did more than just cloak her injuries; they were declarations

of allegiance to the vision of Mexico that Rivera had for years frescoed across the walls of the nation's capital. Like her husband's, Frida's *Mexicanidad* was revolutionary and communist. It celebrated Mexico's diversity while looking away from Europe towards the country's indigenous roots. At a time when all women in the Western Hemisphere were still meant to aspire to some Anglo-Saxon ideal, Frida rolled her eyes at the bland blandishments of New York fashion. A year after her wedding, Frida toured the US laden with Aztec jewellery; in one press photo, she slung her shawl across her chest as if it was Pancho Villa's bandolier. She wore petticoats embroidered with dirty poems beneath dresses she borrowed from Mexico's Tehuantepec tribe. The Tehuantepec are famous for their sharp-tongued women, who reign as queens in their local markets, and Frida adopted their long skirts and bright blouses as a feminist statement. She pulled her hair from her face, braided it with ribbons, pinned it with flowers, then twisted it up into a crown. Like most displays of authenticity, hers was both made up and true.

Frida and I share the same background—one half European Jewish, one half Latina—and in *My Grandparents, My Parents and Me,* she paints her Mexican grandfather as a brown-skinned, indigenous-appearing man. But she was not Tehuantepec or Tehuana, and photos pre-Diego show her as the sleekest flapper-girl ever to grace modernity. Frida claimed her share of indigenousness at a moment when all of Mexico's elite was doing the same, in the service of the same nationalist and revolutionary identity. Pity is, if she

lived during Social Justice Tumblr era, she'd probably be flayed online for cultural appropriation.

The thing is, Frida lived too richly for the shallow pieties of our time. I loved her since I first saw her as a little girl, dragged by her father to the Museum of Modern Art. Her lacquered self-iconography drew me in. I loved the iron of her stare, the sensuality of her body, the queer defiance of her moustache and unibrow. During university, I fell in love with her again when I watched *Frida*, Salma Hayek's biopic. There she was, printing communist manifestos one minute, the next twirling the ravishing photographer Tina Modotti through a tango, then finishing a bottle of tequila in one swig. Glamour, leftist politics, sex, danger, fame. Art above all else—rebellious, meticulous, surreal. Frida was and did and tasted everything. How could anyone not long to do the same?

Thanks to *Frida*, every art girl knows the contours of her life. Diego's affairs. Her affairs. Josephine Baker. Leon Trotsky. Diego's mural chipped from the wall of Rockefeller Center at the orders of Rockefeller himself. Diego's expulsion from the Communist Party; Frida dutifully quit afterwards. Diego and Frida's fervent readmission to the Communist Party. Their divorce. Their remarriage. The amputation of Frida's leg; ever intolerant of ugliness, she wore a high-heeled prosthetic, painted red and decorated with bells. Her triumphant solo art show, which she attended despite her doctor's orders. Her death, too young, in too much pain.

Since this is a story about fashion, I should perhaps talk

about how her style evolved over the years. Instead, let's look at one last item of dress. We've studied the medical corsets Frida painted and the indigenous costumes she wore to express an identity only partially hers. Let's look, lastly, at her bed.

You may not think of her bed as a dress, but what is a dress except the garment that wraps around you, concealing and ornamenting you at once? For a woman as ill as Frida, is a bed any less than that? Frida's bed shines as a magnificent work of self-expression. She worked in bed on a custom-made easel, painting her portrait from the mirror her father had fixed to the underside of the canopy. Embroidery edged Frida's pillowcases; she decorated her headboard with photos of Diego, Lenin, Engels, Stalin, Mao and Marx. By the time movers pried Frida's bed, with Frida in it, from her room and hauled her to her first solo show, the bed was a swaying mass of politics, personal quirks and artistic beauty. Like the corsets, like the dresses, the bed became an extension of her body.

In the seas off of Indonesia, there lives *Camposcia retusa*, a crab that decorates itself with sponges, shells and rocks. Scientists can strip off the crab's ornament, but a crab of this type will, said one witness, 'immediately begin to clothe itself again.' For some creatures, beauty becomes an exoskeleton. Accretions of art and fashion transform humans into icons. They protect a vulnerability far deeper than the pain that seems so easily flaunted—something no one has any right to see.

Frida is gone now, but Frida is also forever. Her art hangs in museums, sure, but so are her more personal creations. In her blue house in Coyaocan, her bed is just how she left it. Her corsets are on display. She lives, still, as the patron saint of rebel girls who long to paint pain and don armour, who reproduce her face in countless iterations.

What if the million Fridas aren't kitsch? What if they are shrines?

Chef Atul's Bandana

CHANDRAHAS CHOUDHURY

Once again, the China Dragon was in a crisis, what with Chef Vishnu having to depart double quick when his wife suffered a stroke in Varanasi. The Dragon was like a body without a head, which is what an eating house is without a chef in the kitchen.

'Don't worry, Vishnuji, we'll take care of everything out here,' I had assured him, as I drove him to the station. 'The captain of a team must know how to play in every position. I have seen what you do and I will work in the kitchen till you return. Maybe it will help me lose some weight. You concentrate on your wife.'

But after two days of sweating above the wok like a pig, I was more than ready to return to the counter as the conductor of the Dragon orchestra. What's more, it became clear from conversations on the phone with Vishnu, who after twenty-six hours on the train had reached Varanasi, that his wife wasn't going to get better any time soon and he couldn't be expected to return for a few more weeks, perhaps a few months. Even maybe never. Dutiful to the last, he said he would speak to his other friends in the Chinese industry and arrange for a replacement chef from somewhere. Sure, at such short notice he'd be no Shah Rukh or Salman, no one to set the cash registers ringing and customers breaking down the door of the house. But in our situation even a Jackie—sorry, Jackky—Bhagnani or a Harman Baweja would do.

The next day when I arrived at 10 a.m. with the day's shopping, all ready to kill myself once again for the sake of the business my father had left me, I found somebody there already. A well-built, dark man of medium height, young but already balding a bit at the centre, not bad-looking, especially with the way his mouth turned up at the corners of his boyish, guileless face, was sitting on the parapet in a faded shirt and trousers.

'Pala sir?' he said. 'Some friends of Vishnuji at the Jade Buddha in Sakinaka sent me. You want a Chinese chef?'

'That's right,' I said. 'What's your name?'

'Atul.'

'Atul what?'

'Mandal.'

'*Arre moshai, tumi Bangali ki?* Are you a Bengali? How many years have you been in Bombay?'

'Seven, sir.'

'And where all have you worked?'

Atul stuck his tongue into the corner of his mouth and began to count on his fingers. 'Shanghai Corner in Kalyan, Wok Star in Chembur, Apoorva Manchow in Borivali, Superstar Shezwan in...'

'Okay, okay, that's enough.'

'Always in Chinese restaurants, sir. That is my specialty,' said Atul with a sweet, shy smile.

'Well, what're you looking at me for?' I said. 'You're hired. Put on this apron and cap and get to work.'

'Right now, sir?'

'When then, on my birthday? Yes, obviously right now! Salary is eight thousand. Industry standard. Probation is two months. After that, we'll see. I can't promise anything. Right now I need a chef, and you need work. Let's leave it at that.'

'Okay, sir.' The lad seemed so pleased I almost regretted promising him the highest salary among the staff. But the chef is the engine of any restaurant; a couple of thousand extra in his pocket was rarely wasted.

'Sir, can you give me a copy of the menu?' said Atul. 'I would like to read it and to give my suggestions.'

'Get to work first, and we'll listen to your thoughts in a week,' I said. 'What? You want the apron, but not the cap?'

'No, sir,' said Atul, reaching into his pocket and bringing out a large piece of cloth with green and yellow checks.

'Oh. A handkerchief.'

'Not a handkerchief, sir,' said Atul. 'A bandana.' Like Lata Mangeshkar confessing that she always ate two warm gulab jamuns before she sang a song, he added with a sweetly mischievous smile, 'I cannot survive a single day without wearing this.'

Well, cap, handkerchief, bandana, pagdi, helmet, who cares? What matters is what the chef puts on the plate. Right on the dot of eleven, the first order came in. Dragon chicken, three plates, *tabadtob pathwa*. Atul had already made a survey of the kitchen and declared himself satisfied with things. But there is also a social aspect to life in the kitchen. In that small space, five feet by five feet, he would have to learn to get along with his chopping assistant, with Mansingh the dishwasher, with the waiters sticking their heads in and trying to pressure him to deal with their orders first. Anyway, all that was for later. The first test was the dish our man put out. Just from the taste of that, we would get to know all about the power of his hand and the promise of all our futures. Like a king sending a message to the royal kitchen, I asked Pintu to ask Atul to make a bit extra and bring it out for me to taste. Sure enough, alongside the three takeaway boxes there arrived a small plate with four bits of batter-fried chicken, artistically framed by a squiggle of oyster sauce, with bits of burnt garlic clinging to them, chopped dhaniya sprinkled on top, and a little pat of chilli flakes in oil in one corner. Red, green, greasy, even a bit scaly, he had indeed summoned a dragon into the borders of a plate. I dug my fork in and sunk my teeth into the chicken. The flavour hit, and went straight to my brain, bypassing a hundred tough and dry dragon chickens of the past like a marathon runner on the final sprint. This was a really talented lad! Why was he out of work? If everything he made tasted like this, perhaps Chef Vishnu would be out of a job when he returned. I ate the surprise snack slowly with real pleasure and satisfaction. With every bite, my mood—a combination of signals from my stomach and promises from my future—became ever more sunny.

Like a bug on a leaf, Atul's green and yellow head appeared from behind the kitchen door. The bandana made him look much younger, almost like a poor man's Victor Banerjee.

'Sir ... is it okay?'

'Hmm,' I said. 'Not bad, not bad. Welcome, Chef Atul, to the China Dragon. We have done our first piece of work together. The next order has already come in. But sit down and have some tea.'

'Work is worship, sir,' said Atul piously, in the great tradition of chefs on their first day of a new gig. 'Give me the orders. I can always have tea later.'

*

In the coming days, I began to learn more and more about the peculiar nature of Chef Atul. Most restaurant chefs think and behave and cook like workers, automatic, years of practice worked into the very bones, chugging along like a Bajaj auto or Sumeet mixie. But this man behaved and cooked like a poet or an artist. Appearances had been deceptive. Behind that sweet face lay a somewhat gloomy soul, even a bit depressive. Atul moved in with the waiters into the staff accommodation, but did not become friendly with any of them. Even after a week, nobody could tell me much about his past. He did not drink, but I was told he liked to go out late at night to Worli Seaface and sit by the sea, staring into the dark of a Bombay night. Once the need to make a good impression had faded away, he dropped all pretence of cheerfulness. But who says the chef has to be a clown? The main thing was that his cooking was often inspired, even sublime. He knew his way around sweet and sour, salty and bitter, umami and my mami, and from soups to starters to main course everything he did was of a certain standard.

Central to Atul's self-conception and his will to work seemed to be that strange handkerchief ... um, bandana. Once he wound it around his head and pulled the knot tight at the back, he was all pepped up like a Mohun Bagan player, ready and focused for the demands of the day. He treated the kitchen like a battlefield. Even without saying a word—and he could say plenty when the mood took him—he was the noisiest chef I have ever known. Bheed-bhaad, ding-dong, thaash-thoosh, all day long. If any of the other staff got too close to him, he lost his temper—not a small problem, in a kitchen as small as ours. 'If I smell your balls,' he used to snap suddenly, 'how will I smell the food?'

But the important thing was that our customers liked the food and frequently praised it, much more than they had with Vishnuji, God bless that poor fellow labouring to take care of his wife. Some folk whom I only used to see once in a blue moon took to dropping by every week or two. Further, Atul was a proactive personality. He reformed the system of making stock and showed me a different system of doing market. He did not waste any expensive ingredients and if anything looked like it might be left over, he made sure to whip it up into something and have it sent out to the biggest table of the night, 'compliments of the chef'. These little freebies and treats go a long way in making people come back, especially us Indians.

Most chefs like a break or two in the day, and unless they're working in an Udupi or pav bhaji place they usually get one. At the China Dragon, of course, there were plenty. Even though the daily takings soon improved by about ten per cent, sometimes there were no orders for a whole hour and we were used to it. But such occasions affected Atul terribly. It was as if the people of the neighbourhood were rejecting him personally. After fifteen minutes, he'd take off his bandana—a sure sign that he was on his way down—and go out and sit on the parapet and smoke, brooding like a thunderstorm. Once or twice I tried to engage him in light conversation at such moments to help pass the time, but he was so curt with me it was almost disrespectful and a different boss from me would have surely taken *khunnas* about it. He was really a very moody fellow, this Atul.

*

Every businessman must have not just employees, but friends—people who are willing to come to your aid at short notice even if there's little gain in it for them. One such fellow in my life was Shivaji, a man in his forties—maybe he was even pushing fifty—who had worked for my father since he was in his teens, and now worked in an Udupi restaurant in Tardeo. Whenever we were short of a kitchen boy, I called Shivaji and he would arrange things in such a way that he did double time, one shift at the Dragon and one at his other place. A man of few words, but with a ready smile—my father used to call him '100-watt bulb'—Shivaji enjoyed my highest respect. Now that things were picking up at the Dragon, and the amount of cutting and chopping and marinating had increased—Chef Atul insisted on making all his own sauces from scratch—I'd end up calling Shivaji at least once a week. Of course, it made for an even bigger crowd in the kitchen. But any person who lives and works in Bombay and complains about crowds should be dumped into the sea.

Anyway, Shivaji. One morning I came into the restaurant to find a simmering tension in the air. Almost the mood of murder, like there was on the streets during the riots of 1992. Chef Atul was sitting at one table, his face as tight as a mask.

'What's wrong?'

Shivaji came out of the kitchen and said, 'Sir, I have never crossed you in all these years. But today it is different. Either he goes, or I go.'

I looked across at Chef Atul. But, like Sanjay Dutt in *Vaastav*, he said not a word, and continued to look out into the distance. I had to call one of the other boys out to get the real story. Apparently, they had all been working in the kitchen, joking and laughing, except, of course, Chef Atul. At some point, things got a bit out of hand and Shivaji had tugged at the knot of Atul's bandana, making it come undone. This enraged the chef so much that he had grabbed Shivaji's throat, nearly dragging him down into the pot of boiling stock. In the war of blows and curses that followed, several plates were broken, as also the Chinese soup-spoon given to me on inauguration day by the restauranteur Keshav Pujari. Such things can never be allowed to go unpunished at a restaurant. They encourage indiscipline, and make the staff take sides instead of working as a team.

But who exactly was at fault in this case? Shivaji, for provoking the chef, or Atul, for overreacting? And even if I wanted to censure Atul, could I risk losing him? If he was someone who could be brought around by talking, there'd be no problem. But he was as sulky as a child; he'd only retreat deeper into his shell. Finally, I just decided to say, 'Such things happen all the time. Let's forgive and forget,' and made them both shake hands. But I could tell that the staff were all on Shivaji's side. Later, I took Shivaji aside and explained that Atul was an unusually sensitive man, especially about his bandana. It was only a small mistake, but circumstances had made it a big mistake. That evening I took Atul aside as well, just before closing time.

'Chef Atul, about this morning...'

Already I could see his mouth tighten.

'Don't get angry. In an industry like ours, you can't have a strong and silent personality like yours. And if you do, then okay, never mind. But work on it a little. A little warmth, a little love.'

'First you tell me, sir. What business did he have pulling my bandana?'

'Chef Atul, Chef Atul ... you know that there is nothing but the highest respect for your bandana in this establishment. What more can I say? Things happen sometimes. The important thing is for life, which is hard enough as it is, to go forward in an atmosphere of love and friendship. I am going to leave it at that.'

But I knew I wasn't making any sense to him. Love and friendship just weren't Atul's thing; he had been born under the house of Rahu. Anyway, in the Battle of the Bandana, Shivaji had the last laugh. He had said nothing at all, realizing that in this fight he had much the weaker hand—there are millions in this city who can cut and chop at the speed of light, after all, and he had a daughter who was studying in Government Law College. But when I called him in again on Saturday, he arrived wearing his usual shirt and half-pant—and on his head, an enormous, ridiculous, crimson top hat that he had found lying around somewhere.

He said not a word to Atul, but to the other boys he declared, 'Just as Mansingh has his special cutting chai, lads, this is my special cutting hat. I always wear it to work. If any one of you jokers bumps into me, it is sure to fall into the stock pot, and then I won't be responsible for what happens.'

And he spent all morning with the hat on his head, while Atul and the stock both simmered silently by his side. The joke swiftly caught on. Soon all the kitchen staff, and even the waiters, had acquired some special item of clothing that they held to be essential to their trade. All of a sudden, Atul's bandana was almost the most mundane style accessory in view. Dharam acquired a gold chain with a locket that opened to reveal a picture of Sonu Nigam, Body Builder found a furry kind of scarf with little elephants on it, Pintu a belt with a dragon buckle, and even Mansingh, the little devil, found a red headband and a pigeon feather to stick into it, like a Nepali Krishna. The whole restaurant became like a kind of fashion show. Crazy stuff. I don't know what Atul made of all this, but then he was the one who had started it all, so how could he now say anything about it?

Wait, did I mention that every time I held a staff meeting, I first put on my clip-on earring?

*

'Sir, I have to tell you something.'

'Yes, Atul, what is it?'

'From the thirtieth of this month, I'll be taking ten days off.'

'Ten days! Whatever for? It's less than two weeks away.'

'Sir, I am getting married, sir. My parents have found a girl for me back in Bengal.' Atul smiled his sweet smile and the dimple appeared in his cheek; it had been a while since any competition to Dimple Kapadia had been seen in Bombay.

'You're getting married? Well, that's a surprise. I didn't even know you were single, chef, you're so secretive about your life.'

'Yes, sir. I am now thirty-two years old. My age is getting on and my marriage has to be done. They have been telling me this for many years and now they have found a girl for me. So I'll quickly go, get married, and come back in ten days.'

'I'm sorry, Chef Atul. You can't go.'

'Sir! Why not?'

'Why not? You've only been working here for three

months, with your regular weekly off, and already you want *ten* days' leave? Who is going to look after your work in your absence? Where will we get another chef from?'

'Sir, I'll look around and arrange for somebody. I only just got the news about my marriage, else I would have brought someone in already.'

'No, that won't do. We are in October and coming up to high season. People have become used to your hand. This restaurant needs to put in a good run if it is to survive and prosper. We have all seen very hard days here. You are part of the team—a big part. You need to put the team first. You can get married any time. Chef Atul, you've waited all these years, so wait six months more. Leave on the first of April and I myself will organize a procession to accompany you singing and dancing all the way to VT station. That's a promise. Only six months of hard work and good business, and then your honeymoon awaits.'

'But sir!' It was clear that Atul had not anticipated his wish being rejected, the arrogant fellow. 'I want to get married, sir!'

'So who's refusing you? But there's a time and a place for everything. Take a bit to time to get to know the girl. Tell your parents *ki rishta pucca*.'

'No sir, I have to go! It is an arranged marriage. There are many grooms in the locality who are younger than me. The girl might not wait. I will lose a wife.'

'Well, that's just your bad luck then. What sort of wife would that sort of girl make anyway? Is a groom a fish, who gets stale in two days? We have to stop this culture of blackmail in our country. Don't stand for it, Chef Atul.'

Atul was so stressed he took off his bandana and began to scratch his head. 'I *have to go*, sir.'

'You *have* to? Well, okay then, go.'

'Oh, thank you, sir!'

'But then it's all over for you at this place. You can find a new job.'

'No, how can you do that, sir! I need a job if I am to get married. I have presents to purchase for everybody in the family, money to give to my parents, things to buy for–for her.'

'It's your choice. If you work another six months you'll have plenty of money saved up for all that. I'm sorry, Chef Atul. I don't think I'm being unreasonable. You can't work someplace for just two months and want so much leave. That's just how it is. Life is about give and take.'

Atul's face had become as black as the face of Kali, only the red tongue was missing. He turned and went back into the kitchen without a word.

*

How you work when you are feeling unhappy or frustrated is one of the biggest tests of character of any human being. To Chef Atul's credit, he passed this challenge. He continued to cook to a very high standard. If anything, the resentment even fed his sense, the way his bandana did, of being a suffering artist lost in a storm of emotions. He went even further into his shell. Everybody knew something was wrong, but not what, exactly. Only I knew that. Deep inside, he was so mad that he gave up even on the few sentences he could be relied on to say during the day: 'pass the pak choi', 'the cleaver is not clean', 'not like that ... like this!' 'move, move a bit further away from me, my head's growing hot'. Rather, he began to reserve his words for Bengal. During the afternoon break and in the low period just before closing time at 11 p.m., he spent a lot of time pacing the area in front of the restaurant like a panther in its cage in Jijamata Udyan, speaking in a low voice on the phone. James Bond was 'the man with the golden gun'; Chef Atul became known in the neighbourhood as 'the chef with the golden bandana'. Sometimes he'd even sit on the parapet, smoking, and staring into the phone with those limpid eyes of his. Maybe his parents had sent him on WhatsApp a picture of the girl who was to be his bride. I'd have loved to take a look at her too, and participate in his sense of pleasure and anticipation. After all, pleasure shared is pleasure doubled. But I felt that he would not take kindly to any moves like this, for it was I who stood, in a way, between that picture turning into a living, breathing person. It would not do even to acknowledge the existence of this problem.

Like a husband and wife who are fighting, we stopped even looking each other in the eye.

*

It had been a long, hard, hot day. The shutters had been downed halfway to show the restaurant was closed, and inside the boys were hungrily eating the dal, bhat and sabji Atul had prepared for staff dinner. I looked up from my accounts.

One plate of food was untouched. Under the shutter, I could see a white-sleeved hand and cigarette hanging down from a body sitting on the parapet.

'Chef Atul, why are you not eating dinner?'

'I'm not hungry.'

'You have to eat, Chef. Come, your food is growing cold and everyone else has nearly finished. I will sit with you.'

'Didn't I say I'm not hungry!'

'Chef, enough is enough. We have to get to the bottom of this. For the last ten days, I have been watching you. How long can you hold a grudge about a matter that is already past?'

'It is not past, sir, the matter is not at all past!' Atul shouted. He turned to look at me and his eyes filled with tears. 'Sir, try to understand! I am only an eighth standard pass—a flop kind of person. But my parents have found a girl for me who is a BA pass! She has a job as a clerk in a shipping company and makes the same salary as me every month ... eight thousand. Her walk and look is tip-top, just like a city girl. When she wears a saree she looks like a living Durga. For some reason, she has agreed to marry me. But her father is ill and they say he does not have much time left on his clock. If I do not go right now and say they must wait till April, they will surely marry her off to someone else. If she knew me, knew what I feel for her, yes she would wait. But she does not—that is the problem! Even if I call them now and say that I am willing to get married at the end of the week, they will agree. Let me go, sir, let me go! Give me half my salary for April in advance and let me go. I promise

I will come back and work day and night. I will be your slave for as long as you want.'

'Now now, Chef Atul...' I said, trying to scratch out something that had got stuck in my eye. 'Such talk does not become a grown man. But if things are that desperate, I will surely not stand in your way. When do you want to go?'

'Really, sir? Are you sure?' Atul jumped off the parapet in excitement.

'Are you going to make me change my mind again? Go on, call your parents and say that you are taking the train tomorrow. That will put an end to their worries and they will sleep well tonight.'

He became as giddy as a little boy. 'Sir, sir, come look at this picture, sir.'

'Yes, let's see what she ... but Chef Atul, this is a picture of yourself, posing on the beach, wearing your famous bandana!'

Atul grinned mischievously. 'This is the picture that convinced her to marry me.'

I became merry as well—after all, who doesn't want two virgins to come together in love, and sex—and, diving back in beneath the shutter, shouted, 'Listen now, brothers! Good news, good news! Our chef is getting married this weekend. Soon you'll all have a bhabhi to cook for you and darn your shirts. Who's going to run down to the store and get us a bottle of Old Monk?'

That night, we had a great party, singing, dancing, cursing, jesting about cocks and cunts, pulling open the *naadas* of imaginary pajamas and petticoats, mast mast, the works. For once, Chef Atul had managed to do something that made everybody happy for him and him happy to let everyone in. Perhaps in the future this could become a genuine brotherhood of men. Then again, it wouldn't do to go too far down this path. It seemed like Atul did his best work when unhappy. It'd be best for the China Dragon if his wife turned out to be an absolute dragon herself.

The next afternoon, after cooking up some truly terrible stuff in the morning—sticky noodles, lumpy rice, vegetables stir-fried into blackness, dim sum spongy like a bridegroom's balls—Chef Atul, beaming like a circus clown, slung his patched-up bag over his shoulder and tucked his two-litre bottle of drinking water under his arm, and, with his wedding advance and other savings securely stowed in his inside pocket, jumped onto the bus for VT station. We were all at the bus stop to wish him goodbye.

'Good luck, Chef Atul! Are you sure you haven't forgotten anything?'

'No, sir!'

That evening, Mansingh, whose day it was off, came running into the restaurant clutching a square of green and yellow.

'He washed it real good last night and hung it out to dry, and then this morning...'

'How will he survive a day without his bandana?'

'Forget it, guys! When a man hears the call of his banana, naturally he forgets all about his bandana.'

*

The news was on at night and suddenly it became interrupted by breaking news. Seven coaches of the Howrah Mail had derailed near Purulia, only two hours before the train was to reach Kolkata. The train had been going at nearly 70 km per hour and there had been many casualties. Sixty people had already been declared dead and the number was expected to rise. Those who had near and dear ones on the train were to call the railway helpline if they hadn't heard from them. A list of the deceased began to scroll on the news.

My heart stopped beating and a lump formed in my throat. Surely whoever is in charge of the affairs of this world couldn't have been so cruel as to ... I saw the name Atul Mandal, age 32, pass by once, and then a second time.

*

For many days, we kept Chef Atul's bandana, without which he really had not been able to survive a single day, around in the restaurant: hung up in a knot above the kitchen rack, folded up on top of the speakers, even under the telephone, as if an order would come in first thing in the morning and he'd tie it up and get to work. All new staff were told about its owner, and how much he had loved it. It became almost a sacred object, like a kalash or a moorti. Some people actually prayed before it every day.

Then, just like the man himself, one day it disappeared and was never seen again. That's just how life is.

William Morris in Balipara

Janice Pariat

I imagine him there.

Bulbous nose, frenzied beard, wild hair, but kind, kind eyes.

Strolling around this one-horse town, a Victorian gent—poet, activist, textile designer—suitably attired in elegant frock coat and top hat.

Amidst the cow carts and fruit sellers, the tiny hardware and grocery stores lining the single main road that runs through this blink-and-you-miss-it urban settlement. I follow him past the small post office and primary school, the one bakery and mithai-samosa shop, heading down a side lane towards a hole-in-the-wall place with light that streams in through one large window. Cloth cuttings litter the floor like leaves, fabrics drape the chair and table, and the sound of a sewing machine steadily studs the air. He is there to meet Swapan, the tailor, and I see that they greet each other as old friends.

In the late 1980s and early '90s, from when I was about three to eleven, we lived on a tea estate twenty minutes away from Balipara, in Assam. Balipara was our closest 'town'. Though we didn't have many reasons to frequent it—procuring our goods and groceries and rental VHS tapes mainly from nearby Tezpur, one of the largest townships in north Assam—we did often drive past Balipara on our way to visit friends posted at other tea estates, sometimes stopping for a snack of roasted peanuts, or quick emergency grocery stock-ups. The one time we did intentionally venture there annually was to see Swapan.

Swapan Das was our family tailor. A petit man, with light bird-like gestures, a wide smile, and wholesome moustache. He stitched cool cotton shirts for my father, light-as-air garments to combat Assam's heavy heat and humidity, salwar suits for my mother, trousers for my elder sister and for me, over the years, an array of beautiful birthday dresses. Sometime mid-December, armed with ribbon and lace (bought in Shillong, or gifted by my grandmother who went on trips to America), swathes of fabric picked from Tezpur's United Traders store, and a number of my mother's old British *Woman & Home* magazines, we'd pay him a visit.

'This one, Swapan,' I'd say, pointing excitedly at a page featuring a dress that had caught my fancy. And he would study it with utmost seriousness, taking in each design detail. The folds and fitting, the neckband ribbing and hidden side seams, the centre front panel outlined in lace, the wide pleated sash bowed at the back, the delicate peek of ribbon, the buckram that gave the skirt a puffy little-girl lift. Then I would stand solemnly upright to be measured. Arm to elbow, elbow to shoulder, and across. Round the chest, and waist, the tape dangling to just above my knees. The numbers jotted down on a notepad, squiggles and figures all adding up to a sum of me.

In a month, Swapan would appear at our bungalow, with the almost completed dress for a fitting. A nip here, a tuck there. The sleeve a little less loose, the hem slightly higher. And it would be whisked away for another week, and returned, in time for my birthday at the end of January. Then, the magic, for me, lay in the mirror, how the outfit would transform me into (what I imagined) a fairy-tale princess. But I see now how the magic also lay in the man who stood patiently behind me, pins and measuring tape in hand.

For the longest time after, we didn't have the need for a family tailor.

In the early 2000s, my father retired and my parents moved back to Shillong, where alongside the traditional bespoke establishments also burgeoned newly opened stores stocking ready-mades. My sister moved to the UK, where getting anything tailored was impossibly expensive. And I drifted between London, Shillong, New Delhi, in and out of employment, which then consequently determined whether I was shopping for clothes at export-reject-filled markets like Sarojini Nagar or branded stores like Benetton. Quite quickly, the malls came. As did the international brands. Marks & Spencer, H&M, Promod, GAP, Zara, Mango. The easily recognizable markers of post-liberalization. And I was, admittedly, not quite the reluctant consumer. In London, especially, as these brands were most easily available, even if not easily affordable.

Only when I returned to India in 2015, did something of this consumer pattern change.

I discovered saris. Cotton saris.

And the rows of emporiums along Baba Kharak Singh Marg in Connaught Place where they were available. Along with other places, of course, including Saree Centre in Khan Market, Dastkar in Chhatarpur's Nature Bazaar venue, the changing stalls at Dilli Haat. Buying saris led to the necessity of having falls and blouses stitched. So, over twenty-five years later, living in Delhi, a city as far away as anything could be from Balipara, I find myself another 'family' tailor. Mr Khan, or 'Masterji' as he prefers to be called, who owns a shop in Uday Park Market. He is soft-spoken and polite, and is patient with my faltering, hesitant Hindi—unused especially to explicating sartorial requests. Nagma Fashion stands towards the end of the market, a space partitioned into a backroom where his assistant sits and the front with his counter, a tiny fitting cubicle and shelves lined with bales of cotton fabric and spools of shiny gold-trimmed lace. He is unhurried and meticulous. When I stand there, getting measured, arm to elbow, elbow to shoulder, and across, I often think of Swapan, and all that these two gentlemen, across time and geographical region have come to stand for: resilience, community, gentle fortitude.

It isn't a realization easily gained.

But oddly enough, one that is spurred to cohesion by an assignment submitted for my art history course in 2016. My student had written a paper that attempted to connect 'Slow Fashion' and William Morris. Could there be a link, I wondered, between the two? For those familiar with 'Slow

Food', 'Slow Fashion' will ring a bell. It's a term recently coined by Kate Fletcher, Professor of Sustainability, Design, Fashion at the Centre for Sustainable Fashion (CSF), University of the Arts, London, and refers to a growing trend within the fashion world for ethical clothing. Just as 'Slow Food' stands in opposition to 'fast food' mass-produced food that is prepared and served quickly, 'Slow Fashion' is a movement of designing, creating and buying garments for quality and longevity. Slow Fashion encourages slower production schedules, fair wages, lower carbon footprints, and (ideally) zero waste.*

What intrigued me was that despite its seeming contemporariness, this wasn't entirely a new idea. Its roots may be said to stretch back to late eighteenth-century Britain, when the Industrial Revolution was at its height. Bolstered by free market capitalism unhindered by governmental supervision, the Revolution wreaked social and economic havoc, the consequences of which were faced mostly by the poorest of the poor—hellish working conditions, unplanned urbanization, squalid, unsanitary living conditions. Amidst this turmoil, though, arose the Arts and Crafts movement that was 'born of ideals'.** At the time, factory production transformed the traditional rhythm of the labour force, which came from agricultural and craft backgrounds. Many of the unemployed or underemployed were skilled workers,

---

*http://study-ny.com/slow-fashion/

**http://www.vam.ac.uk/content/articles/t/the-arts-and-crafts-movement/

such as weavers, whose talents and experience were suddenly rendered useless given the 'efficiency' of the new textile machines. It was a loss of far-reaching magnitude—with a severance, violent and brutal, between nature and labour, between objects and hands, between life and seasons, between people and sense of community. The Arts and Craft Movement grew out of a concern for this. For the effects of industrialization on design, traditional skills, and the lives of ordinary people. It established 'a new set of principles for living and working ... advocating the reform of art at every level and across a broad social spectrum. It turned the home into a work of art.'* More pertinently, social reformers such Walter Crane, John Ruskin, and William Morris believed that good design was linked to the notion of a good society. A vision of a society in which workers were not brutalized by industrialization, but rather could take pride in their craftsmanship and skill.

My choice, I realized, of where to shop for clothes, and what I choose to wear, even day-to-day, was not merely one of taste and affordability, but of ethics. Was I doing my part? How should I proceed? I felt the only way I could learn was in the past. In the life that William Morris led.

He was marvellously multitalented, of course, skilled in a wide range of crafts including printing, typography, book binding. (To him we owe a vision that influenced the evolution of design as we know it today: that of linking art to

*http://www.vam.ac.uk/content/articles/t/the-arts-and-crafts-movement/

industry by applying the values of fine art to the production of commercial design.) Yet I found inspiration in his words.

In a lecture delivered before the Trades' Guild of Learning on 4 December 1877, he laid out ideas that he felt were important in his creative approach. Guidelines that remain pertinent—within slow fashion, and elsewhere in the design world—even today.

'Our subject,' he says, 'is the great body of art.' (Which includes trades of housebuilding, painting, joinery and carpentry, smiths' work, pottery and glassmaking, weaving, and many others.) Everything made by man's hands has a form, which, according to him, must be either beautiful or ugly. 'Beautiful if it is in accord with Nature and helps her; ugly if it is discordant with Nature and thwarts her; it cannot be indifferent.' I find the idea incredibly moving. That decoration must not be guided merely by the craftsperson to work in the way that Nature does, 'till the web, the cup, or the knife, look as natural, nay as lovely' as their real-life equivalent, but also to place ecological awareness at the centre of creative practice. To not be discordant. To not thwart with our dis-compassion and thoughtlessness.

If we extend the metaphor to include consumers, it bears on us not to be indifferent to what we purchase and from where. It's a lesson I'm trying to put into practice by being mindful of certain things before a purchase. From where are raw materials sourced? How are the artisans treated? What ethical production practices does the brand put in place?

In his speech, Morris also encouraged the 'study of the

work of the ages of Art', by which he meant that artists need look to the past for their inspiration (believing that the art of his own age, mutilated by industrialization, was inferior). He felt that this would enhance the quality of life for all, and that artistic activity itself would be seen as a force for good in society. In this guideline also lies a reference to the appreciation of art history—to acknowledging, and learning, from the way things were done in the past. Far from being a call for sentimental nostalgia, this becomes imperative to our contemporary times of rapidly disappearing traditional craft practices. And, on our part, to support the initiatives of those clothing companies that do.

We're mostly all familiar with the story of Fabindia, for example. Established in 1960, by John Bissel, an American businessman who ran a handloomed-textile export business in India, Fabindia is synonymous with supporting traditional craft techniques and skills. Anokhi, in the 1970s, was founded in Jaipur by conservationist J.P. 'John' Singh and his spouse Faith Singh. And in the initial years, the focus was primarily on reviving 'Rajasthan's traditional techniques of hand block-printing that had lost local relevance'.* Most inspiringly, Anokhi serves as a viable business model for the revival and continuance of India's traditional crafts. Recently, there are more success stories to be recounted. Sanjay Garg, for instance, the designer behind Raw Mango, a brand of contemporary Indian handwoven textiles using

*http://www.thehindubusinessline.com/life/2003/12/15/stories/2003121500020100.htm

traditional techniques. An unbeliever in fashion shows, and working largely with Chanderi, Benarasi and Ikat craftspeople, Garg affirms in interview after interview that Raw Mango products are designed with 'the intention of bringing together traditional weaving skills and modern design sensibilities.'*

Apart from an awareness of our art historical past, also central to the Arts and Crafts Movement was beauty. Feeding, of course, into the time's ideas of *l'art pour l'art*—or art for art's sake—that expressed the belief held by many writers and artists associated with aestheticism, including Oscar Wilde, that art needs no justification, that it need serve no political, didactic, or other end. But beauty also that wasn't shallow. Ruskin, Morris and others advocated for individual craftsmanship to be revived—to allow workers to produce beautiful objects exhibiting the result of fine craftsmanship, as opposed to the shoddy products of mass production.

Workers, the reformers believed, could produce beautiful objects that would enhance the lives of ordinary people and at the same time provide decent employment for craftspeople. It's a link we should be trying hard to sustain, even, perhaps especially, today. And while the critics cry that usually exquisitely made and decorated pieces can only be afforded by the wealthy (it's true), my focus lies on strengthening ties elsewhere. On supporting, as practitioners of slow food do, the local. 'Eating local' is a geographical concept related to

*https://yourstory.com/2011/02/sanjay-garg-founder-raw-mango-on-being-a-fashion-entrepreneur/

the distance between food producers and consumers. To adhere, as the Slow Food website suggests, to the thirty-mile or even the 100-mile diet, which isn't a long-distance weight-loss programme, but the radius within which people should try and source the majority of their food.

Similar with craft. To find, as often as you can, carpenters, tailors and other craftspeople who live around you, in your own or nearby neighbourhoods. Sourcing locally sustains local economic well-being, helps to foster a sense of community.

Often, at Nagma Fashion, I am amidst other clients who have been visiting Masterji for years, with their mothers, and now their daughters. There is jovial conversation, a rare camaraderie, much joking and teasing. Masterji is more a gentle father figure than a tailor.

In my years living in the UK from 2011 to 2014, I noticed two things.

That the consequences of the Industrial Revolution ripple on. In the way that the British have largely destroyed their own craft traditions. From an island thriving with lace makers, wood workers, weavers, blacksmiths, basket makers, calligraphers, among others, they're reduced to subsisting on cheap 'Made-in-China' imports. Of being corporate, multinational, brand-dominated. Of anything handmade being relegated to the realm of notorious expensive inaccessibility. It's a path I hope India will not take. Though all hope is not lost for the UK. The Arts and Crafts Movement also quietly lives on. In fact, there seems to be a resurgence in the appreciation, and the making, of things. In an article in

The Independent, reporting on 'the spectacular renaissance of arts and crafts in Britain', Rosy Greenlees, executive director of the Crafts Council remarks, 'There's been a re-engagement with processes and a desire to reconnect with our physical surroundings. It is linked with the issue of consumption and an awakening interest in provenance and authenticity.' In 2011, the V&A presented an exhibition called 'The Power of Making' dedicated to celebrating the 'role of making in our lives', including an eclectic selection of crafted objects, ranging from a life-size crochet bear to a ceramic eye patch, a fine metal flute to dry stone walling. In literature, there is a return to nature of another sort, memoirs of making as it were, such as Robert Penn's *The Man Who Made Things Out of Trees* (where he cut down an ash tree to see how many things could be made from it) and Peter Korn's *Why We Make Things and Why it Matters: The Education of a Craftsman.* 'Every man-made thing,' he says, 'be it a chair, a text, or a school, is thought made substance.' Online, websites such as Etsy, which offer peer-to-peer e-commerce, focus on handmade or vintage items and supplies, are burgeoning with over fifty-four million members.

And moving back to India has helped me notice parallels.

Handmade, organic cosmetics grow increasingly popular, as are (if the number of adverts popping up on my Facebook and Instagram feed are to be believed) stores, both online and off, selling handloom garments, including Rust Orange, Runaway Bicycle, Lila, Nicobar, Jaypore, Bhane. It is exciting because as Garg says, 'We have textiles like no other country.

We use textiles not as luxury but as a necessity.' On my part, I'm determined to buy more handloom fabric, tow them to Uday Park Market and have Masterji stitch them into garments. To travel, and source locally from the places I visit around the country. To support the emporiums which, as far as I can tell, don't receive much footfall. To attend craft bazaars. To gift people presents that have been handmade, or that I have handmade. As Steve Wessel, a flute-maker says, in the V&A video accompanying 'The Power of Making', 'I think craft, or working with your hands, is fundamental to being human. Making is life.'

Back in Shillong, my mother recently rummaged through a trunk containing old clothes and fished out my birthday dresses. Still lovely, still almost new. She's taking them with her to the UK for my sister's daughter. They will be passed on. Swapan has created heritage. Garments adorned with memories and much love. His subject too is the great body of art.

Undressed

Rosalyn D'Mello

It was dark outside by the time she had woken up. The earth had turned and the light of dusk had begun to dissipate. Her eyes were still drowned in sleep, but she knew she had to swim nearer to the brink of consciousness. Too much was at stake.

Naked still, she wandered towards her living room and stopped at the wall facing the chaise longue, the only site in her apartment that housed a timepiece. She could just as easily have opened her laptop, but she preferred not to contend with the deluge of unopened mail that she knew lay sitting in her inbox, nor did she want to glimpse at her cell phone, lest she be distracted by unsolicited text messages. She wanted the isolated gestures of two hands striding a circumference so she could gauge exactly how many hours she had at her disposal until it was time to get dressed. If the season were more fixed, she would have felt little need for such evidence. But the continuing light chill set the climate in a liminal zone between the end of winter and the beginning of spring; an in-between region where the days were neither too short nor too long; where the presence or absence of light did not denote chronological exactitude. The bigger, more intimidating hand, was inching towards three, while its smaller counterpart remained steady at six. It was early enough to suffice, but that didn't mean she had time. She had promised to meet him for dinner at eight. She was regretting this commitment. It was beginning to assume the burden of an obligation.

At the time—just two days ago—she had been swayed by his persuasiveness. But today she felt differently. It was already becoming difficult to retrace what about him evoked her curiosity. It was possible, she thought, to blame it on her hormones. It'd been three days since she had stopped bleeding and her body was currently in heat, like some beast howling in a frequency audible only to her. Her cunt needed to be petted and caressed; subsumed and swallowed. It was hungry.

She had done it again, referred to her cunt as an *it*; as if articulating the feeling she had had of late, of her cunt being something that belonged to her and was yet separate from her, like a sentient being with its own peculiar, particular subjectivity. 'Lust for emotion'—she suddenly remembered reading that phrase a week ago in one of Woolf's diary entries.

If her cunt could speak, she wondered what it would say. If it had to be christened, she wondered what name it would go by. Angela? Teresa? Sosostros? Medusa? Kali? If only she could annotate her body the way she did the books she read. Inscribe, erase, illustrate. Stick post-it notes around the region of her thighs, for instance, to remind herself to trace their long surface more regularly. Her body had recently become a source of endless fascination and she remained in awe of everything it could conjure for her upon her summoning; the immense pleasure that lay nestled within her, like a book of prayers customizable for every intercessory occasion.

She sought the annotations also because they could offer easy access to her barrage of potential lovers, who could check on movements against her skin without having to check in with her. She could be pleasured without having to give away the keys to her ecstasy. She could remain mysterious and yet be satisfied, without surrendering too much of her self. She could remain unto her self and yet yield to the power of suggestion.

Focus. She had to focus. If she bathed now, she would have enough time to make her self up. She could try that new shade of plum on her lips. She would be more efficient if she laid out her clothes first and then went for a shower. What was she to wear, though? She had in mind a dress, but she suddenly detested the idea of any kind of fabric encasing her body. A skirt would tug too tightly at her waist and reveal her residual cellulite. Hers was not a 'perfect' body, her breasts flopped a little and her belly was closer to a Khajuraho relief than the proverbial Size 0 model. She loved how the contours of her stomach curved above the beginning of her bush. She enjoyed outlining the arc of resident flesh. It lent substance to her body that had grown up too skinny and conservatively, devoid of any excess or indulgence. She was not embarrassed by it, but she knew he would notice her bulge and that he would judge her for it, not knowing how beautifully it presented itself unclothed, unencumbered by the veneer of fabric. She wanted to be shameless but was surprised to learn she had become cautious instead, too afraid of allowing her body to make any heated overtures. If she wore something too skin-revealing, she could seem presumptuous. She wanted guarantees. She had trained herself to only respond if there was sureness; and to only ever respond, never more to initiate, not unless she was convinced of reciprocity. She was obsessed with shame and yet found herself wary of it. Yes, that was what she wanted now, most of all. No more virtue. No more experimentation with grace. No more subscription to monasticism. She would, henceforth, be shameless by embracing the mortification of shame.

As she stood in front of her cupboard, nursing her newfound revelation, she thought of the beginning of O's ascent into abjection, when her lover, Rene, escorted her in a taxi to a house in Roissy. What was it called, that house? She struggled to remember. She had the book with her. It had recently been returned, her copy. Where had she kept it? It was in the bookshelf in her bathroom. She paced towards it, still naked, and looked through the three shelves to the right of the commode. She had bookmarked the page, which was unnecessary, she now realized, since it was right in the beginning, but there were all those pages preceding it, the preface by Pauline Reage's lover, who pretended not to know her identity, but who, it was later revealed, was in fact the person who impelled the book's becoming. He had challenged Reage, or the woman who called herself Pauline Reage, saying something about how no female author could compete with the eroticism of Marquis de Sade's stories of desire and debauchery.

There it was. They were about to reach the house, he was about to instruct her on how she must behave when he drops her off at the front door, how, if she didn't obey immediately when she was let in, they would force her to, when he continued with his undressing of her:

'Don't move,' Rene says. 'Sit perfectly still.' His hand reaches for the collar of her blouse, unties the bow, then unbuttons the blouse. She leans forward slightly, thinking he wants to fondle her breasts. No. He is merely groping for the shoulder straps of her brassiere, which he snips with a small penknife. Then he takes it off. Now, beneath her blouse, which he has buttoned back up, her breasts are naked and free, as is the rest of her body, from waist to knee.

By now she had moved involuntarily from the bathroom to her bed. By the time *they proceeded to strip her till she hadn't a stitch of clothing left, then put her clothes away neatly in one of the closets*, she was wet. Concentrate, she chided herself. She was lying flat, her legs splayed, the fingers of her right hand already having slipped within. She was wet. 'Wet,' she thought, 'what a wondrous word.' So suggestive of liquid on the threshold of spilling over, but not quite liquid enough. The middle finger of her left hand rested in the niche of her navel. She wondered why it was called navel-gazing, this act of looking inward. There it was, her navel, so obvious, with a depression deep enough to whisper secrets into. She remembered a lover who would in fact speak into its depth, then flutter her eyelids over the gorge as if sealing it. She wondered what if, all these years later, she could shovel them out and sift through them. In those moments when Sabina used to softly breathe into this cavern, she never thought to ask what she was mouthing, what dark matter was being buried inside this orifice to be gated by eyelids. But now, all these years later, now, when Sabina had long since surrendered to the conformity of a middle-class lifestyle with its predictable humdrum, she wondered if her once-lover had invariably ensconced within her a fragment of her soul; the most uninhibited shards that at the time felt shameful. Were she a painter, she would create an outline of her body's form in charcoal and have tendrils growing out of her navel, like the blossoming of something magical and mysterious, like when plants mushroom from seeds scattered by the migratory movements of birds.

Focus. She needed to focus. She was meandering. She didn't have too much time. She should have come by now. She should have been dislodged. Why couldn't she just get off watching porn? Why did it make her so uncomfortable to see nude bodies writhing in a choreographed frenzy? Why did she have to be so damn cerebral about the whole business of affording oneself pleasure, as if there were a limited stock of available orgasms, which meant she was compelled to make each one count? The supply was countless, she knew, and her capacity for ecstasy would only/could only, expand with age, and there was no such thing as a wasted orgasm or an inutile one. They were all useless. Dispensable and infinite.

*

How to speak the body erotic? How to declare the constitution of the erotic, when one is no longer defined by sexual pursuit? When one has (inadvertently) claimed the superiority of the celibate? When one has come to be in possession of the cellular knowledge that men are small and passions short lived? I did not intend to/did not set out to eliminate sex from my daily existence, but I do not grudge my body its present inability to seduce. There are more immediacies to heed to than those particular to my body. For example, how must I receive from the cosmos the gift of fiction when for so long I have been wedded to the scripting of my self, to autobiography? As I inscribe this menstrual minstrel ('Why is it so difficult to write?' Cixous asks in her essay, 'What is it o'clock?'), my yet unnamed, somewhat unknowable protagonist is lying in her unmade bed, wading in a different whirlpool, one of her own lust.

*

Let me not mistake my delay for lack of urgency. The truth is, I am still beside myself. I was temporarily incapacitated. My body had become blood fruit. And all I knew during the lifespan of the week that came before, my only experience during those seven-eight days, was one of painful anxiety.

I refused to feel defeated. I made several attempts—all

in vain—to inhabit my body while simultaneously feeling detached from it. On the one hand, I was nursing a minor wound that was healing, that was flesh-pink, that was new skin, the region around it still peeling, old skin being shed in the aftermath of a cooking scald, a reminder that an immense burn can also be regenerative, despite the ensuing soreness (softness of tissue). On the other hand, the expected trauma of blood continually streaming from my womb.

I wondered briefly about the precise moment of so much bludgeoning fullness that the blood finally begins to drip-drop, my womb's passive-aggressive tantrum; a spiteful admonishment for my not having made allowances for impregnation; for permitting the on-going barren refrain—my preferred, privileged state—of continuing childlessness.

Is this to be my fate? This unasked for, uninvited shedding of endometrial lining every 24/26/28 days, until (at last) at least two-and-a-half decades later, it finally runs dry? As if all my purpose was contained in this isolated, solitudinal gesture, this nursing of a wound that perhaps marked the beginning of time? Did Eve menstruate before or after she ravished the forbidden fruit? Is this menstrual condition a punishment meted out to womankind for her alleged transgression? Why is it that, despite my will, my being must reduce itself, periodically, to its biological essence: preparing itself as a reproductive vessel, demand to be seeded so it can yield flesh, so that the (possibly undeserving) species may multiply?

Is blood the opposite of strength?

It is one week later. It is 4 a.m. I have woken up because I can sense my cup has runneth over, an emergency leak. I walk to the bathroom of the ostentatious suite I am co-habiting with my lover, who is sleeping. I need to replace the cotton lining my panties with another. Everywhere I go I carry with me the smell of iron. And even though I changed, three hours later I woke up to a crime scene. Blood on my thighs, blood on the sheets, blood on the floor, blood continuing to flood out of me as I rushed once again in the direction of the white-tiled bathroom. I must carefully undress myself to contain the bloody exodus. I place each item in the white sink and turn on the tap so that the cold water gushes over the stains. When I raise my head, I glimpse at my face in the mirror and discover hot tears of shame. I feel exactly that which I am now—unclean.

*

My period interferes with my intuition. This presents a problem, considering that, increasingly, I know that the only solution to the question of writing is to hone one's intuition (the intuitive self, the intuited self, the connection between cosmos and self, a welcoming of synchronicity, mystery and magic). A kind of clairvoyance. And so, when I menstruate, I find my body struggling with the environment around it. I bang my foot against the base of the bed. I hit my wounded finger by mistake. Period brain: this tendency towards an unconscious inelegance. I can't remember her identity, but there was this woman I'd met once, who spoke about how she was so attuned to her body, she could control its secretions, she could decide when she wanted not to menstruate and her period would go away, simply abating itself. She could control the tide, which meant she could control the moon, which meant her being had cosmic resonance, which meant she was obviously bullshitting. Unless, perhaps, she was something of a sorceress, with fingers that could heal or curse depending on what she desired. If, indeed, she existed, and I haven't invented or imagined her, then I would like to meet her to correct my wrong, my very grave error of not having asked her before how she was able to exercise so much power over her body. What was her secret? How had she mastered her intuition so that it was more authorial?

*

'I'm sorry, I couldn't do what you asked me to. I started writing, suddenly. It was like a gush,' I told my lover over the phone one afternoon (in almost summer, when I was beginning to ripen yet again).

'For you, blood and writing always seem to come in a gush,' he said, laughing.

'It's true,' I said.

Later that day, I copied down this excerpt from Cixous's essay*:

It is very nearly the end. It's very nearly life.

Extend the hand, write, and it's all over with the end.

*'What is it o'clock?' *Stigmata: Escaping Texts*, Helene Cixous.

Writing is the movement to return to where we haven't been in person, but only in wounded flesh, in frightening animal movement to go farther than far, and also, effort to go too far, to where I'm afraid to go, but where, if you give me your hand, I'll endure going.

*

Writing (/Onanism) is (are) not defined by hand gestures. It (they) involve(s) the dressing and undressing of situations, consciousness; a general (sporadic) undoing of the self.

It is imperative that you learn that she, my unwieldy protagonist, never makes it to her date. She saw ahead of her two choices: to cease her endless fantasizing, to quell her urge to dip in and out of textual arousal so she could bathe and prepare herself for the endless possibilities contained by the night; or to continue with her navel-gazing, her self-stimulation, her journeying into regions of previously unimagined ecstasy. I chose to address (redress) my wound (womb), leaving her to her will.

*

Her onanism was uncontrolled, like a plot-less narrative leading to twists and turns, with no ostensible direction but a clear destination. Even the entity of a climax was unfixed. She could see them as a series of pit stops, of undoings and becomings, a general diaspora of waiting and birthing and cessation of life and then a baptismal regeneration; body being body but conscious of its soul-ness, its in-corporealness that exceeded its dimensions that poured outwardly into the universe but was not contained by it, like a stream of water being endlessly poured into a shape-shifting vessel that could and could not hold it all so it spilled over but did not contaminate the naked floor, instead caused wild roses to bloom instantly in the contours of its spill so all that she would ever be was a patch of earth that ploughed itself, that feasted off the immediacy of its environment without dangerously consuming it, that bred life, that was seeded by a multiplication of warmth and lust and emotion and the lust for emotion, and the unbridled, shameless pursuit of ecstasy; a pièce de résistance against the consumptiveness of the un-feminine world. By pursuing only the unholy cause of her appetite, she could deliver the world from its misery. Within the secret vicissitudes of her cunt lay the salvation of humankind. While many among her species wandered uncertainly and busied themselves with the monotony of earning a living, evangelizing the gospel of capital gains and fiscal returns, she would lie here on her unmade bed, in her deformed nakedness and take upon herself the guilt of civilizations, the burden of all the violence that was ever inflicted on fellow men and women and all the shame that had ever been felt and all the volume of songs that had never been written and all the complexity of unabridged sorrow and unhappiness that anyone anywhere had ever felt within them, and she would take it all in to her hands and roll it along her fingers so it could be shaped and re-formed and she would slip it inside her until she could shove it past the fangs of her labia and plunge it inside her so it would melt, along with her own darkness and her unrevealed anxieties and insecurities and vulnerabilities and she would twist it in harder and faster and for longer each time until it reached her very core and met with her throbbing pulse, compelling it to knock faster against the shores of her almost wail—then her wail—then a birthing cry until it became liquid, like her, and metamorphosed within her and became part of her but also something separate and elemental, and so when she would let out her final cry, for a heartbeat of a second the universe would cease to grieve for its eventual demise but would be restarted, reset, and everyone would experience a moment of amnesia followed by a second of joyous ecstasy—a collective baptism, and even though, after the moment would have passed and her sigh would be let out, the world would return to the way it was, it would be different still. It would be mysteriously anew and unchartered. And when it would invariably go to seed again, she would repeat her miracle so that the mortal world would be delivered once more, and again and again and again, for eternity.

Sorting

VLADIMIR LUCIEN

I learn to spend Saturday mornings
gathering his week in soft crowds of fresh-
smelling cloth, purging his pockets of:
receipts, coins, paper-money, folded notes,
just like Mama did for Daddy—Daddy who
she used to shower her could-do-no-wrong love on.
I spend Saturday throwing his dirty shirts,
pants, jeans into piles, heaping them into small
can't-take-no-more mountains—separating, sorting,
carrying each load like a new and sour pregnancy
in front me to the new machine (that Daddy could've never
dream of buyin' for Mama). That machine with its cold
white body, its lights and buttons, its troubled-waters
sound. The first day I used it the whites came out
from it shining like denial. Then, the other moved
mountains of his things: bending
my back and gathering, gathering, gathering—
the ups and downs, darks and brights. The true
colours. The delicates. The blues.

WITHOUT A STITCH

VAYU NAIDU

Ko Na Rak finished his overnight care duty from a secluded apartment in Mayfair. It felt surreal walking through the cobbled alleyways of Shepherd Market because no one in this part of town looked like an employee; at least not in Social Services. They all wore lounge jackets and jeans at 10 a.m., hanging around a doorway painted in cobalt blue, not quite summing up the Georgian Pub's name, YE OLDE GRAPES. They were all hooked in making deals on various devices. Around the corner, smokers in these parts took to the sheesha or e-cigarettes while waiting or baiting bids overseas, across time zones, or face to face with each other, speaking in English with foreign accents. This was the unfamiliar face of Britain.

Unwinding into downtime was what Ko Na Rak had waited for, and was fast blurring into a dilemma of choices. He headed for the ordinary Caffe In in the square. Three men with their backs to him were seated across the long tables diagonally. Their padded shoulders tense; their heads lined by the violet glare of their laptop screens. They were downing time as if it was on tap. Ko Na Rak smiled thinking up the scene as a piece of performance art, which he would review as: 'An installation of head-and-shoulders featuring minimal movement in minimalist space as millennial collective art consumption–this is great contemporary choreography post Ecocrash.' He smirked at his pratty cleverness as he merged ecology and economy in his reference to the 'Crash', which was a daily reality for most Britons.

On his return from the unisex toilet, he discovered that the men were looking intently at their screens for the new Autumn selection of Menswear. These guys really had time between deals and look deadly unapproachable, he thought. This was an ethos so different from his current training in the Social Services. In working with vulnerable people, he had wanted to specialize in mental health of Elderly Care. His mates often joked that it was because he was *Asian* British he seemed to be embedded with a culture of engaging with an assortment of elderly relatives and their needs. While it was joked about, it was admired and not without a hint of envy. He enjoyed the banter and that's where the politics of identity would emerge between his culturally hybrid mates and him. But he had not bargained for the night duty shift system, and as a trainee he did what he was given. He wished he could make time with his mates during the day, and yes, browse and talk about everything under the 'lunar sun'–in other words offload their wishes and woes till infinity. But his time of signing off in the daytime, his proximity to the City, or Guys & St Thomas's Hospital where most of his mates worked, made this impossible for the next six months.

A debrief with his colleagues once a week was the next best thing if they could afford the time. In Britain's time of austerity, no one complained about the absence of downtime even if it bled into additional hours of care. The NHS and local authorities had been the jewels of this democracy's taxpayer with Social Services; but the financial crisis axed jobs and eroded lives. For Ko Na Rak, it was always a relief to be at work and it was a greater relief to be able to walk away from the smell of loneliness that papered the baroque interiors of his client's spacious apartment. It was a release to know that he *could* and did care.

At the moment, though, his dilemma was simply figuring out what the hell he was doing standing in a place which sold nothing else but innocent stimulants like sugary tarts. And he wasn't even craving for a sheesha or caffeine. However, he needed a necessary distraction as part of his intensive overnight while he was on duty with his client Quinton who was consumed by dementia. The dementia had grown like bindweed choking the cognitive functions of his patient's short-term functionality. In the past, Quinton had travelled the world and was a renowned Antiques Collector of wood and bronze from South and East Asia. But now, it had become an hourly ritual for Ko Na Rak to open the gaping wound of the man's inchoate present to remind him how to eat. He did this by holding an antique food bowl in front of him. The rationale advised was that it would trigger a memory of the past when Quinton, who had forgotten his name, could relish every cuisine of food. Ko Na Rak massaged Quinton's jaws for him to chew mechanically. Then coaxed him to swallow the food without choking, and this could take the whole night till daybreak when Quinton slept. When the coral velvet curtains were drawn slightly for Quinton's view of his tree in the garden, Ko Na Rak would look at the iron railing on the western wall where a sixteenth-century Varanasi brocade sari would glow when the sun caught it. It gave him a warm wave of cultural pride that this was among Quinton's rare and personal collection that his eyes gazed on and took comfort. It evidently had story, but the teller was silenced.

Here, in the cafe, Ko Na Rak's gaze fell on the face of one of the men facing the screen. *Click*—eyes glazed—*click*, total intoxication as something desirable flashes. Then the curl of the nostril and lip. Code: contempt, *Click*. Furrowed brow even more tense, then leaping up, in a hurrah! of met expectation. Ko Na Rak peeked. It looked like it was a choice between the Filipe Fatouzi bomber jacket—*scroll down*—or the Balmain sheepskin jacket. The dilemma was resolved in the man-staring-at-the-screen's face. Ko Na Rak would never know if it was a choice between texture, style, or price. The man zoomed on the 'window dressing' to the backdrop of the model. Billowing chiffon saris, each a colour of rainbow, cascading from the old wooden doorframe, trailing from the exhaust of the Harley Davidson, flowing from a terracotta urn perched carelessly from a window in the Moroccan streetscape. For Ko Na Rak, what the jackets had in common was the colour of sheepskin and sand, the cut with hand stitching, revealed at the outer seams. The stitchless flow of the saris gave the men and their jackets the toughness, with a hint of tenderness.

Ko Na Rak was luckier than many. He could afford to dress the way he liked and live within his orbit of ethical global issues. He wasn't a campaigner, but he knew he had earned enough to turn to what he wanted to be recognized for: caring. It wasn't about awards or accolade, but to be a well-dressed man from body to heart and back. Now that he could afford it, he had enrolled on a well-meaning part-time Master's in Cultural Studies at UCL. He attended his classes one evening every week and have time to study between his care duty which were four night shifts, and one training day. It also meant no downtime with his mates.

Study was the necessary distraction, as something was happening in his life to replace something else that had happened. He often talked to himself in such abstractions and realized that if he was to be turning in an essay, he had better deal with the grit of specifics; 'illustrate your argument with case studies' as his tutor remarked on his submissions. His phone alarm bleeped—downtime had run out. Now he had to get on with the day. He smiled at the woman at the counter, as if to say 'Oops! I only used the loo this time—will be back for coffee and cake—tomorrow?', and she waved smiling through her bright red lipstick at him. She was Polish, a reader of facial expressions, with very little English, and knew his shifts.

He had appointments waiting for him at home or was it homes—dilemma again—Dad and Mum's at South Ken, or his own at Shoreditch? His think cloud featured some graphics of home-cooked food at Mum's—branded as HOME BASE.

That was the determining factor for this fond and itinerant son. Letting himself into the corridor lit by the garden that flanked the reception hall trailing the aroma of cardamom, he smiled to himself, thinking; '*Love your food, Mum, it's just the chatter I can do without! So much for my ambitions in caring, huh?*' His think cloud even had an emoji winking, but full of heart. What a relief no one was home yet, and a reassuring feeling that before long they would all assemble around the kitchen countertop. A barstool was draped with a pleated and pinned turmeric-coloured sari. 'Stitchless and standing, another title'. The frig door was splattered with Post-its scribbled with lists ranging from cleaning agents to prohibitively priced wine lists.

He enjoyed telling himself that this singledom was soon going to have a companion. On the counter opposite him, in the LED frame–his Goddess with a cheeky grin looked directly at him. Rekha. Ray as he called her, as he winked back. It was her idea to go retro Indian with the B&W photograph and a twist of diaspora–glamorously studio lit, but without the bordered sari or jewellery. Instead, it was the Jaeger 2013 quilted bomber jacket, the way he had seen her the first time they met. Multiple versions of Rekha Ray kept emerging in the frame in a photoshoot of five settings–in a haveli garden, wearing a pink leheriya dupatta; a lean-to in Zakynthos in a tee that merged with aquamarine sky and sea; a paddy green Mysore georgette sari at a friend's wedding in Auckland; a purple dress suit by the Lion at Embankment. Ko Na Rak's mum and sister liked these as a talking point with visiting friends and relatives. His favourite was Ray in Jaeger's bomber jacket and bandini salwar with boots. She was his girl, woman, everything. He had never wanted to marry, but then, one day, his grandfather changed his life.

Ko Na Rak remembered the ninety-seven-year-old held his hand—reaching out as he had done a millions of times over the years. 'Better get married'. The old man's voice purred like gravel under soft shoes. It wasn't an order. Instead, it had the certainty of a man who knew the best about his beloved grandson. Ko Na Rak stroked the wrinkled skin of the old man's hand that looked like crushed velvet the colour of shimmering gold. Following his grandfather's funeral, he announced to the family that he would marry, but it was purely a matter of his choice. His father, mother and sister backed off in an instant, as they stood in a semicircle, flashing smiles like paparazzi cameras, watching him wipe his tears that day, and in the days that followed.

The quiet of the house washed with memories. He placed the lamb biriyani saucepan on a slow, sustainable heat. A pending tutorial assignment and its viewing list prompted him to watch the film he had set on the flat screen in the kitchen.

Click—and Guillermo—the icon of Interculturalism, performance artist in the 1990s, took over the screen. His handlebar whiskers pointed in the direction of the sun, or north of the border. Around his theatre-set kiosk were dressed chickens. There was a joke about the word 'undress'; for humans it 'means clothes off'. But for chickens 'dressed' means with feathers off. The audience in the dark, of this now grainy live recording, laughed in spurts signifying they understood the subtext. Guillermo was dextrous in illustrating assumptions from dress; he was dressed in a Bomber jacket as a contemporary Bandito. Laughter from the audience responded to the accents he could switch between. American University deconstructionist, anthropologist, to Mexican labourer fleeing across the border, to US police border force paranoia, to Ivy League dinner party guests, to TV anchorperson and reporter north of the border. During his live performance, with the dressed chickens as puppets, he was the puppeteer of the strange case study of Little Red Riding Hood.

The protagonist puppet was a sausage. Dressed in a red handkerchief manipulated as a hand-held puppet, Red Riding Hood spoke Mexican and the language of the consumed to a consuming silent chorus of dressed chickens ready to be stacked on cold supermarket shelves with an assortment of stuffings beside them. And, sage and onion along with chipolatas and varying lengths of pork and chicken sausages were among these with bold placards that read 'Try me!'. Ko Na Rak released a loud cloud of laughter at this audacious and stirring voice of performance art. The politics of Red Riding Hood as a national border state being radicalized with the red handkerchief was alarmingly clear, with hindsight; relevant then and now.

For Ko Na Rak, it was the dress and undress that took the central metaphor. It was sexy as politics, while it referred to unvoiced oppressions that happened daily and globally. Guillermo signified the politics of Mexican poverty then and it was relevant now; for Ko Na Rak it identified the wall of race and class he knew from childhood. The assignment had opened the can on brands; he was no Lichtenstein, but he could spot satire and his grandfather's love had made him discern between authentic feeling and fake. He used the inheritance from his grandfather for the Master's. So, with art affecting his little life, why was he so taken by Ray in her Jaeger bomber jacket c. 2013? He and she had gone to an exhibition titled UNDRESSED: A Brief History of Underwear at the V&A. Near the grainy B&W photograph of George Bernard Shaw wearing Jaeger's early endeavour at hygienic men's underwear. They read about the writer's dilemma: would it be more unfortunate to be forgotten, or, to be remembered primarily for modelling underwear rather than one's vast literary output? It made both of them laugh too.

For Ko Na Rak, Jaeger, Guillermo, or any brand were beginning to signpost the politics of identity and perception as being dressed and undressed. So, what was Ray's statement about wearing the bomber jacket that appealed to him, and what was the symbolism that filled his dear and scatty mother's heart about Ray wearing the sari? What had struck Ray and him about the early Jaeger was the evolution of hand-stitched clothing to the uniformity of the machine stitch. It was also about cutting animal skin or woven cloth in compartments for sealing from cold, or for morally, and hygienic reasons to define limbs and body parts. Ko Na Rak was playing with words. Instantly he decided his essay would be on the legacy of the sari among British Asian Diaspora. Materials and culture.

The front door clicked open, then slammed shut. The creamy quiet of the house was swallowed as different pitches of his family's voices streamed in. Shopping energized them and they gathered around him completing each other's sentences. He listened, between mouthfuls of his heated biriyani, of what his mother had planned as the wedding menu.

*

Autumn went by in a blaze of bonfire nights and Diwali celebrations despite Brexit. Ko Na Rak and Ray found new hope with London's new mayor and a world city they belonged to which was a long haul from their parents' generation. Now Asian—rather, subcontinental was serially hip across the FTSE too. Saris were back in fashion at events and worn with flair by cross-cultural women. Saville Row too boasted of a new window of talent. Italian fabrics selected by its Indian owner-designer was now employing English cutters for the best Nehru jackets in the world that made 007's costume designers think again. Ko Na Rak was to go for fittings there, which was once again surreal after his care duty; Quinton could barely eat floating on clouds of memory in Asia, Africa and Australia, suggested by the tapestries and objects that surrounded his bed.

The wedding was scheduled for August next year. His mother would host regular meetings with him. She would arrive at his flat in Shoreditch with at least five saris at a go for him to approve of that were to be given from his, 'the boy's side, to Rekha'. He had grown up seeing his mum in trousers and jackets or at most a salwar kameez for weddings and funerals when he was a child among other Asian mums and his mates. The sari was a new phenomenon and he was unfamiliar with the length, breadth, texture, colour, if it were woven or synthetic, and how to tell from the stitch or the pattern, its regional origin. He indulged his mother's barrage of details that she had acquired via social media, her all-knowing sister, friends, trips to India and Bangladesh and her keen sense of business to set up a sari salon in a quieter London off Chelsea's Kings Road. She was also his informant for that essay that was now turning into his dissertation. When she paused for breath at their sessions, she would prompt him: 'Well? What do you think?' Tactile as his nature was, it didn't take him long to start unfolding the saris. His task was to imagine Ray in them and that wasn't too tough an assignment. It became a visualisation of texture that draped over form. Some saris were so sheer, even the embroidery, or lace, or sequins, or brocade did not interfere with the sheerness of its fabric.

'So smooth,' he would say, stroking an embroidered chiffon sari against his cheek. His mother's scowl at the possibility of the sari getting puckered in his stubbly beard was enough to make him do it more. 'But it's seamless!'

The image of draping the fall of the sari seemed to give him undue licence to the imagined female body, the landscape of his wife-to-be and he shuddered at this spur of territoriality he found in himself.

'It's unstitched too!' he couldn't help exclaiming.

'Arre! That's why it can be used for so many things. Hanh! By the rich and the poor. For us Indian women, of a certain age, it is our lifeline, our childhood and memories of becoming brides. Even when we are taken to our cremation. It's our second skin.' Unexpectedly, she buried her face in the red checkered Kanchipuram and sobbed.

'Memories, dear, memories with the saris given to me by your father's mother and mine...'

He wiped her tears with his Kleenex and she taught him how to fold a sari, from its long river-like flow to the conciseness of a rectangular fold, the size of a table mat.

Ko Na Rak could see this wasn't about the people she referred to. Somehow the sari had wound itself around the desires of womanhood haunting her with the loss of a supine youth, maybe? He could only guess. Now that a thread was unplucked he wanted to go further and untangle the weave of his mother as a woman in her own right, not just as his father's wife or his mother. He might have to wait.

She gulped down his selection of tea from Borough Market and did a double take—the tea was an excellent blend, but she was also looking tearful after what, she felt, had been clumsily said.

'Now, promise me you will look after Rekha?'

'Don't worry, Ma! I won't disgrace the Asian male, and in return, you must promise not to suddenly transform into 'dragon' lady!' he teased her by waving the embroidered chiffon. She laughed and nodded her head vigorously.

He had taken a fancy to the colour of a ripe mango Mysore georgette; he had to gift it to Ray. It reminded him of a nostalgic song she sang about women drying their saris that stretched like mustard fields till the cow dust hour peeled them dry.

It was June, and perfect sari-wearing weather in London too. The stag night had morphed to include the henna ceremony as well. Both their sets of mates walked in procession in all manner of dress along the embankment by the Globe and assembled to drink moderately at the oldest pub by London Bridge. The sun would set after eight in the evening and their beloved Thames would be glinting with lights across embankments. Ko Na Rak had walked ahead with a couple of his mates to grab tables and chairs and set the tab at the bar. Ray held back by the corner for her friend who, running late after work, was determined to dress and rival the Mango Mysore georgette and they both dared the ghost of Jack the Ripper with a laugh.

Ko Na Rak and Stuart, who was to be his best man of-the-heart, and Deep who was to be his best man of-the-head, were together settling drinks for the others who were seated and scrambling a few more chairs across the wooden floor of this pub. In London, this pub had hosted histories of sailors, politicians, actors, dead and alive. Laughter and thumping hands on tables soon ensued, followed by the decibel from the stereo growing louder after the downing of the first drink. Ko Na Rak relaxed and couldn't hear the sirens in the streets. Time had released the tension of waiting. He could see the creamy ankle of one his classmates as she pulled up her electric blue chiffon sari, winking with sequins, and bent down to fasten the buckle of her high-heeled sandal.

The earth shifted.

Ko Na Rak saw a man rushing in with a machete in one hand and whoever was there by the front door was mowed down and another and another and people were collapsing like puppets. Then the man who struck, ran out. Gut-wrenching screams and blood trailing on the floor. It was dungeonesque. Ko Na Rak found himself lifting the two bodies that had fallen one on top of the other at the front, the way he would Quinton. Stuart and Deep were screaming along with the bar staff to 'GET DOWN!' There were shots being fired in the distance, the sirens of fire engines, the metallic voices over megaphones, and screams. Inside his head, the nursery rhyme 'London Bridge is falling down' was playing in a loop; when he shut his eyes it was Guillermo's dressed chickens. Suddenly Stuart leapt across the floor and tried to get Ko Na Rak down. That's when Ray walked in through the entrance. Ko Na Rak couldn't figure out if she was dragging her friend or if her friend was pushing her. Ray's black hair mixing with her friend's blonde head on her shoulder behind her. Ray in the mango coloured Mysore georgette with the bomber jacket slung over her shoulders.

She walked in and hit the floor on her knees. Ko Na Rak then saw her right side. As if in another world where time had stood still, the jacket slid. Elbow down, her arm had been hacked, the flesh and hand hanging from the bone, her left side with three gashes from stabbing. The drowning of the noises around him and her increasing silence made him wrap the sari around her. There was more unstitched sari he pulled at and he wound the bits of her body that had been hacked, closer like a hammock that women place their sleeping infants in. He smoothed his bloodied hands over her second skin.

She smiled.

Art, life, Quinton, his mother sobbing into a sari, Guillermo's chickens, London by the Thames blown apart, were colliding inside him. Without a stitch, the sari had flowed river-like in his life, cradling body parts and the one love he had found to be discovered again.

Sorry, Mr Chang

Manu Joseph

1

A happy hooker is the end of civilization. Most men like the idea of a cheerful whore, and perhaps the end of civilization, too, but women will not let that happen. They need to believe that working girls are all miserable, that they were all trafficked and fed heroin, that they all have to be saved. If the fallen are not miserable, what is the whole point in not falling?

There is no particular reason why she is thinking about hookers; she is not one, as any informed person who is careful with words will agree. She may have seen some cheap girls on the street as her taxi heads towards the airport. She was probably not even thinking about them. She was only thinking about happiness. She has always considered herself happy, happy in an ordinary, boring sort of way, which is the only kind of happiness that is not a misunderstanding of happiness.

2

When people think of happiness, they are usually in trouble. She is. She has not done anything stupid, and it was not a bad plan at all. She is not an impulsive person, but people who weigh things are not always safe from danger. There are always things you just didn't know to weigh.

3

If she must steal for the very first time in her life, should it be a national treasure, that too of China, and worse, steal it in China? Hong Kong to be precise, but if you get in trouble in Hong Kong then, you are not in Hong Kong, you are in China.

There is a 90 per cent chance that she would get away. But when people express things in percentages, they are not being mathematical. In any case, she has never considered probability a part of maths. Even as a school girl, she could not accept that probability was maths. How can something that is in the heart of half of poetry be maths?

4

She is a beautiful young woman even though she has a high forehead and small round lips. Without make-up, she looks naïve. Just the right kind of naïve, the naïve that is adorable to men. Not a small-town simpleton, in which case she would not be a scalp, but a calm girl with a moral compass. Even men who are not Indian, who cannot see the meanings in the light of her eyes, see her this way. She does not know if this perception is true, and that is not very odd.

5

One of the things she likes about this airport is that it is just called Hong Kong International Airport. There is no person in its name. Left to them they would have just named it Airport. That is how they are here. Surely there is a building somewhere in Hong Kong that is just called Building and a park called Park.

She walks to the Air Asia counter where there is an unhappy man behind the counter who clearly has nothing much to do but he is staring intently at a computer screen.

She wonders if it is good idea to fly to Singapore instead of Delhi. If Mr Chang wakes up in the hotel room and finds his treasure missing, he might be able to get his powerful friends to sound an alert in the airport. All he knows about her is that she is Indian. That is enough to get her, but if things go to the wire, she would be wise waiting at a gate for a flight that is not leaving for India. But then if they track her to Singapore, it would be easy for Hong Kong to get her back.

She must take a chance and fly to Delhi. If everything goes wrong, which is unlikely, her story would still be reasonable: Young Indian girl flees from a Hong Kong billionaire, accidentally brings with her a two-million-dollar Chinese national treasure.

There is a seat on the flight but the airport price is five thousand Hong Kong dollars. She pays by cash but that does not get the unhappy man's attention.

6

At the check-in counter, the girl takes a good look at her, especially her sarong and appears to control a chuckle.

'Ma'am, any bags for check-in?'

'No.'

'Can I see your cabin luggage?'

That is an unexpected question. Maybe they are wary of Indians who are always carrying bags that are too large for the cabin. She shows her the tiny black purse.

'That's it, ma'am?'

'Yes.'

'You are travelling to Delhi with no luggage?'

'It's a short flight.'

'Ma'am, you are travelling to Delhi with no luggage?'

'It's an emergency. I had to leave the moment I got the news. What's the problem?'

7

Her story, if it all comes to that, is that she is fleeing a powerful dangerous man. How can she go to her hotel room and take her luggage? She is fleeing a psycho and taking the earliest flight out of Hong Kong.

Also, if Mr Chang wants to be discreet about how he lost the treasure, he may have to be discreet about what exactly it is. If the alert in the airport is a bit vague and the cops are searching for a thief who is transporting an artefact as large as a table board, a young woman who has no luggage at all would be the least suspicious.

But she did not expect the fact that she does not have luggage to draw attention of the check-in staff, all of whom throw looks at her sarong. If they were Indian, she would have deduced the meaning of their stares but she does not understand the facial expressions of the Chinese.

Maybe they were not looking at her sarong at all. In the circumstances that she is in, she is probably overreacting to simple things. Also, it is, beyond doubt, the most beautiful sarong in the world. Eventually, they give her the boarding pass.

8

She finds a corner seat in a café, covers her face with her hands and appears to cry. That is for the cameras, which are everywhere. She has to be distraught.

When she was in the taxi, before she switched off her phone, she had WhatsApped four girlfriends the same message:

'Just been assaulted by a man. He is a big shot, billionaire or something. Scared. I am leaving on the next flight home. Don't call. I am switching off phone. I am fine. But dazed.'

There is a good chance though that she would not need a story in the first place.

9

She is on her way to Gate 71. Some people, the women especially, appear to look at her with wry smiles. She accepts, though, that she could be imagining things. But as nervous imaginations go, seeing strangers laugh at her is a bit weird.

It is five in the morning. In two hours that plane will taxi towards the runway. If she gets lucky until then, she will be off with a two-million-dollar heist. Maybe Mr Chang is still sleeping.

10

Any moment now a gang of cops could come, point their guns to her head and take her away. It would be embarrassing. Considering all that would happen to her if she is proven guilty, she wonders why she is worried about being embarrassed when the cops take her away. Maybe that is how shy people are; no matter what the hierarchy of their fears is, the fear of embarrassment will never be trivial.

She is shy. Some people would find that hard to believe, and some men would absolutely love to know that.

11

A large middle-aged cop approaches her. He looks like a senior official who may have never had to run in his life. She is almost paralysed with fear. Just for an instant he looks at her sarong. He looks amiable but maybe that is how they do things here. He smiles at her and asks in fluent English.

'Where are you from?'

'India,' she says.

'Holiday?'

'Yes.'

She does not stop walking. She is a beautiful young woman and she has the right to walk away from an amiable potent man. She thinks he is going to ask her to stop but he just walks away shaking his head and laughing.

12

At Gate 71, people are shuffling in a long line to board. It is not her flight. This one is headed to Dubai. She is early, a bit too early.

A flight to Dubai is boarding at Gate 71, but she decides to sit there, in one place, and not move until it is time for her to board. She has picked up a hat from duty-free. This is the best she can do. Still sit and wait. It is highly likely that Mr Chang is still sleeping.

13

She had arrived in Hong Kong two days ago for a regular modelling assignment. The middle management of a well-known real estate brokerage firm was meeting in Hong Kong. In the evening, there were some fun and games for them and she was the mistress of the ceremony. She had to just introduce the speakers and crack some jokes, which most people never got anyway.

When she is on such assignments outside India, she freelances. She has an agent who arranges her to meet chosen clients. She is expensive and not on the regular circuit. She goes at five thousand US dollars for four hours.

14

She went to meet Mr Chang in his suite in the Four Seasons. He said he was Mr Chang. If he was Chang, she was Sameera.

She was wearing a black sleeveless top and a full wrap-round skirt, which she could tell he liked. She looked like a woman he would have won through his charms.

Mr Chang was a slim handsome man of around sixty. He had a full mop of silver hair and twinkling eyes. He was a real estate tycoon, married to an artist, according to the agent. Apparently, he had made a late call in his life, to stray. He had two adult children. This was a man who had much to lose.

15

Mr Chang was cordial. He asked her if she would have a drink. She sat in a chair as he spoke about the only time he visited India—he had gone to Bihar to see Bodh Gaya. 'India,' he said and shuddered. Then he was worried he may have offended her. Eventually he stopped talking and looked around the suite, his fingers drumming his knees.

'If you don't mind, can you please go to the middle of the room?' he said. 'Just stand there please. What I like is looking.'

She stood, he looked. She should not chuckle. That deflates men. She tried to look nervous and unsure. They like that.

He went to the wardrobe. There were many dresses hanging there; all of them looked like uniforms. He picked out a costume and asked her to change.

'This will fit you. It is the uniform of a waitress in one of my little restaurants.'

'All right,' she said. 'But, Mr Chang, no spanking.'

'No spanking. No. No.'

'And no other kind of S&M stuff.'

'No S&M.'

'I just want you to wear some clothes and talk to me. But you have to be convincing. You really have to behave like a waitress.'

'I can try.'

16

She emerged from the bathroom in the red checked dress that reached till her knees.

'Come here, stand next to me. Come here. What is your name?'

'Sameera,' which was not her name.

'It's been an hour since I ordered my soup.'

'Very sorry, sir. It's coming soon.'

'I am very disappointed in you.'

'I am so ashamed, sir.'

'You are incompetent.'

'I am sorry, Mr Chang.'

'Is this how you run a place? I am sorry this is not working.'

'Shall I look more scared?'

'No, no. You please be spontaneous. In the cupboard, there is a police woman's uniform. Please wear that and appear before me. And be yourself. Just imagine you are a cop, and you are here to investigate me.'

17

Mr Chang had not touched her, yet; he was resorting to kinks to stimulate himself. He could not wait until he got bored of her body; he had moved straight to experimentation. It was as though she was not a person but a moment in his long progression with the female body, a moment that contained all his boredom with women, a sum of all the things he has done to them before, like every story is a sum of all stories that have ever been told.

She was not offended. She felt sorry for him. He would always be searching for the perfect sex and not finding it because there is no victory in paid sex and she thinks it is victory that men really seek. Or is it just that the stakes are really low with a call girl? There can be no defeat, no hurt, no pain, no embarrassment, and no tomorrows. She does not know why but men miss something in paid sex. You won't believe that though if you knew how long this whole business has been going.

18

She changed into several outfits. She became a school girl, a serious executive and a doctor but there was something that was bothering him. Maybe he could see through the farce. But then everyone can. It was something else.

'Have you done this before?' she asked him softly. She was wearing a doctor's coat and found it funny that she did sound like a doctor.

'Yes,' he said. 'It is just that none of these costumes make any sense on you. I know there is something that will make you exactly the way I want you. I know I want you on your fours but there is something else you need to be wearing.'

19

She emerged from the bathroom in a pink sari. He studied her intently, then stripped the sari off, leaving her only in her pink blouse and pink petticoat, which she thought was the most inaccurate word in English.

'Please kneel down,' Mr Chang said. She did. 'Actually, please be on your fours. Yes. Yes. Please raise your skirt till your knees. Yes. You are a gorgeous woman. Look at yourself in the mirror. Look there. You are so gorgeous. Your face is fresh, your nape long, your back so strong I can see three muscle groups move, your core powerful and your calf muscles are full. That is the most underrated gift, you know, full calf muscles.'

He walked to her and poured a full bottle of Evian on her back and stared at her lush buttocks as it revealed its form.

'You said no spanking.'

'No spanking, Mr Chang.'

'On what basis do you instruct me?'

'Sorry, Mr Chang.'

'I can give a hundred dollars per spank. All I need to give you is ten.'

She was quiet. He slammed his hand on the wall. 'Just this hard. Not harder than this. Ten, that is all.'

She was quiet.

'US dollars, obviously,' he said.

'All right, Mr Chang.'

'When I hit you, you have to say one, then two, then three.'

'Yes.'

'Oh.'

'What do you mean, Mr Chang?'

'Actually, I do not wish to spank. I just needed to know you would be willing.'

Bastard.

He turned away. 'Please dry yourself, and come sit with me.'

She said, 'Is something still bothering you? Do you want me to wear what I was wearing when I first walked in?'

He was not listening. 'I like you,' he said. 'I don't feel like I am with a, with a, you know ... you are amateurish.'

He looked wounded. 'Did I offend you?'

'No, I think it is a nice thing to say to a woman.'

'That she is an amateur?'

'Yes.'

'I see your point. Sex belongs to amateurs,' he said. 'In every other thing that people do, the amateurs imitate the professionals, but in sex the best professionals are those who can imitate the amateurs, or they make an ass of themselves, gyrating and cow-boy fucking and all that.'

'Do you think I am pretending to be an amateur?'

'No. I think you just are one somehow. Except in one

sense. In everything we do it is the amateurs who enjoy the craft. In sex, too, I am sure.'

'I do enjoy.'

'Let's not bullshit each other.'

'Is there anything I can do to make you happy?'

'You will make me happy. Before you leave this room, I am sorry, you will make me happy.'

'Why do you apologize, Mr Chang? I am here for that. I am not a thief.'

At that moment, he was stunned by an idea. He called someone on his cell phone. Then they waited for about an hour.

20

'It has arrived,' Mr Chang said when the bell rang. 'Please go to the bathroom. My staff will bring it in and they will leave in a minute.'

21

When she stepped out of the bathroom she saw a massive bubble-wrapped object the size of a table tennis board lying on the bed. It was a painting?

'No. A piece of cloth,' he said. 'From another time. It is the most expensive textile material in the world.'

'How old is it?'

'You didn't ask how much it is. That's good. I like that.'

'Honestly, I was going to ask that next.'

He laughed, and began to take the bubble-wrap off. What was soon revealed was a framed rectangular cut of exquisite silk, about five by five feet in dimension attached to a velvet board.

'Is it really silk?'

'Yes, from a thousand years ago.'

On the cloth was a red dragon swimming in a green ocean. And there was something written in black in Chinese, vertically across the work.

'What does it say?'

'It is Cantonese.'

She waited for him to say more but he stood looking at the cloth in a mild trance of affection. It was hard to dislike a man who could feel so strongly about silk.

'This is the largest piece of silk from ancient times,' he said. 'Nothing on earth so old is so big. Every other piece from this era is very, very small, the size of a sleeve or a handkerchief but look at this.'

'How did you get it?'

'I bought it last month,' he said. 'From an Indian who lives in Singapore.'

'For how much?'

It was then that he turned to look at her carefully, indecently, top to toe.

'Two million dollars. Take off your clothes.'

22

As she undressed, he carefully unscrewed the frame, discarded the glass and with very gentle hands removed the piece of silk.

'I have never felt this material before,' he said.

'What do you plan to do with it?'

'You know.'

'Aren't you afraid you are going to ruin it?'

'It is still so strong. It is from the tenth-century Tang Dynasty. It was woven in Sogdiana, which is now somewhere in Uzbekistan.'

'It looks like this cloth was a part of something larger.'

'Yes, it was a part of a banner outside a rich man's home.'

'Not the emperor?'

'No. That's the strange thing. The story goes that he was a thief who had amassed a lot of wealth.'

'That sounds like an emperor.'

Mr Chang laughed. 'He wasn't. Even I don't understand how he was allowed to survive. Many rich homes and palaces and temples used to have giant banners. He had one. Or that is the story.'

23

She stood facing the full-length mirror. The room was dark but for her glowing form under the spotlight. Her breasts were bare. She was wearing the two-million-dollar silk cloth like a sarong.

Mr Chang emerged from the shadows, naked. He stood behind her and kissed her nape softly, then he pushed her back forward with rude power, lifted the most expensive skirt any modern woman has ever worn and, holding the silk, he thrust into her.

24

They were talking in the bed, something about madness and how madness alone has power, and how the world is unhappy because most people are sane and how unhappiness is often the result of sane people imitating the madness of mad people—'Socialism, God, love,' Mr Chang said, 'they are all antique insanities.'

'Love too?'

'Love in its original form is madness. Most people cannot love, they do not even know love. What is generally called love is only a misunderstanding between man and woman. Then they get cured. And they are stuck.'

At some point he dozed off. He did not mean to. He must have been tired. He had already paid her and she could just leave. These jobs end like that sometimes.

The ancient silk cloth was on the floor, stretched to its full length on a rug. Mr Chang, after the fever of sex, had felt stupid treating the two-million-dollar antique with such rough hands, and he really was very rough. He planned to fix the cloth back in the frame in the morning.

She slipped out of the bed and wore the silk, just the way Mr Chang had instructed her to wear an hour ago. She slipped on her top and walked away.

Mr Chang would not want too much attention on how he lost the silk, and might be inspired to keep it all quiet. Maybe she would sell it back to him after she got back to Delhi.

The other possibility is that Mr Chang has a large capacity for disgrace, the most dangerous type of man. He would wake up and find the Chinese national treasure gone and call the police. He would only have the physical description of the girl. He does not know her mobile phone number or even her name. Even her agent does not know her real name or phone number. They communicate over email.

If the police wish they would be able to track her down to the airport and nab her before she flies away. Mr Chang can initiate a chain of legal actions even if she manages to escape. But her story would be this: She was talking to him in the bar of Four Seasons, he invited her up to his room. When he started getting kinky, she wanted him to stop but he didn't and she somehow fled with whatever cloth she could find. And she wanted to flee Hong Kong because he was a powerful man and she would be at his mercy anywhere in the city. It is not a perfect story but it is something.

The best scenario though is for Mr Chang to wake up late.

25

At Gate 71, the flight to Delhi is announced and the boarding has begun. She stands among the shuffling line of people. Another one minute and she would be in the plane.

She sees a policeman talking into a device and approach her. Their eyes meet, she is sure about that but then he looks away. He is about twenty metres from her and there is no doubt in her mind that he is walking towards the boarding queue of the Delhi flight. In the next ten seconds she would know if he is really coming for her.

26

'This sarong,' the woman behind her says, 'I have not seen a more beautiful thing.'

The woman is middle-aged, and Chinese like everyone who has taken note of her sarong.

'Thank you.'

'Did you get it here?'

'It belongs to a friend.'

'Is it old or new or what is it? I don't understand it.'

'It is old. Yes, a bit old. But what's there is to understand in a sarong?'

'It's naughty too.'

'You said naughty?'

'Girl, do you read Cantonese, dear?'

'No, ma'am.'

'So you don't know what is written on this piece of cloth?'

'No. What is it?'

'It says, "I am a thief".'

She giggles. The policeman continues to walk towards the queue. Five, four, three, two...

Confessions of a Travelista

Divia Thani

It was when I was standing, freezing, in a tennis court-sized refrigerator in Moscow that I should have realized I was losing my mind. In front of me, in long aisles, hung fur coats all wrapped up on sturdy hangers, a supermarket of lush mink, fox, sable, chinchilla, beaver, rabbit. Except that these exquisite fur coats weren't for sale; they were simply being stored in optimal conditions—temperature- and humidity-controlled; protected from sunlight, dust, moths—for wealthy Russians during the summer months. (Which, if you're a Bombay girl like me, still feels rather nippy.) These 'fur refrigerators' are essential for correctly preserving such expensive garments. Why was I—a girl who lives in a city where there are only three seasons: hot, hotter and rainy—shivering in a massive basement with blasting air-conditioners on my free afternoon in Moscow?

Because I needed to understand how it worked. Because I wanted to buy a fur coat. That afternoon, despite all ethical issues, I *needed* a fur coat. Frankly, I couldn't understand how I would live out the rest of my life *without* a fur coat. I had spent my week in Russia in work meetings, taking notes, exchanging visiting cards, but really, my mind had been consumed by fur. Every store I walked into, I headed straight to the back, and tried on half a dozen coats until I narrowed in on what would fit perfectly on my body, what matched my hair. I agonized over fox versus sable. Brown versus black. Ankle- versus knee-length.

My travel companion was at first amused, then bewildered, then completely exasperated and exhausted. 'What are you going to do with a fur coat in Mumbai?' he asked.

What is the point of a life without a fur coat, I wanted to retort.

Instead, I tried to rationalize. It's not for Mumbai, I explained. I work in travel. I travel to a fiercely cold destination in Europe or the US at least twice a year. How is a grown woman supposed to look chic while staying warm and toasty? The answer, sadly, is not a puffy down jacket, which suited me fine during my university days. It was no longer my trusted, faithful Donna Karan black wool coat with large buttons that had survived many a New York blizzard. In Russia, where temperatures drop to –15 in winter, fur is unquestionably the easiest way to stay warm and protected. And while it's fashionable, it's also cultural—you inherit your mother's coat, you save for your own first, like it's a ritual. In Russia, they call fur 'soft gold'; it has the magical effect of enveloping you in what feels like a cuddly toy, while sexing you up like a red Dior lipstick. So, standing in that gigantic Moscow basement, I decided to take the plunge. And if that meant I had to go vegetarian for the rest of my life to make karmic amends, and empty out my entire refrigerator to store a fur coat for the remaining eleven months of the year in hot and sweaty Mumbai, well, I was going to have to buy a new refrigerator. (And possibly a new apartment to fit it in.)

Truth be told, this sort of fashion dilemma is not a one-off. It's an occupational hazard. I edit a travel magazine and website for a living, and it involves a lot of travelling across India and around the world. I pride myself on doing it right—I research destinations painstakingly, everything from its history and culture to the food and arts, the high fashion and the street style. I never pack without checking Instagram to see what real women are wearing on the streets that week—it's a much more accurate way of gauging the climate than using a weather app. When I land in a new city, I want to look like I belong to the city. I still carry Indian jewellery and accessories, but the rest of me wants to look like a chic local.

The trouble is, I want to look local everywhere I go. That means I get fitted for qipaos in China, and happily trade them for tiny shorts and loose tank tops in Australia. In Paris, I let my hair dry naturally and my wardrobe goes grey; in London it's all black. In Lucknow, I spent a month's salary (pre-tax, mind you) on buying an entire suitcase full of chikan saris and kurtas because I was convinced I wanted to wear nothing else for the rest of my life. When I returned from Spain, I wore floral scarves over my shoulders for weeks. I have six jade bracelets from Bali that were blessed by a healer. In South Africa, I decided I'd celebrate vibrant colours and bold prints forever—*I mean, what is the point of a life without colour?*

Each new place I visit, I fall in love with. And that's great for my job, because I return full of excitement, enthusiasm, details, recommendations, contacts and story ideas. But each new place I visit, I decide, I have found my long-lost style soulmate. Who knew that I loved dressing just like the sun-kissed girls from Leblon in Rio de Janeiro, all floaty, flirty skirts and touches of gold? A month later, I feel Dubai is truer to my Sindhi soul (short skirts, small handbags, big heels, oversized sunglasses; the only thing sun-kissed are highlights in their hair). A month after that, in Kerala, I decide all fashion is nonsense—nothing compares to the everlasting beauty of handwoven saris. But a month later, I am in Korea, and I am amazed at the sophisticated, cool cuts that even its youngest contemporary designers produce. *What is the point of a life without edge?*

And so, I buy. I collect. I amass. My cupboards spill with trinkets and labels from across the globe, a fashion sensibility that changes with every flight and airport passing. I flip through the pages of *Vogue*, and I envy how they give all these women a thoughtful moniker: design diva/boho chic/corporate cool. And there I am: Indian Born Confused Traveller? A more horrific thought: Does a lack of sustained preference mean I haven't any true style at all?

I don't just dress for places, I let the places I go to dress me. I fall for their quirks and eccentricities, I love the stories behind them. In Brazil, in beach towns, you can get mini-pedicures on the street. No parlours or salons required, just a little raised step on a pavement and you can walk away with your toes painted a sexy fuchsia. But that's Brazil. You must be sexy, always, forever. You must carry a bikini in your handbag. Otherwise you must be crazy. In Kenya, you must be bold in your dressing, you must be fiery, you must tightly wrap fabrics around your head that prove it, you must carry music in your hips, you must be a strong, fertile woman or you will lose. In Russia, you do not see animals as creatures that require protection or pity; you think, first, always, about your own survival. You see fur as necessity, not extravagance. In Lucknow, where the history of Avadh is right in front of you and yet falling into ruin, you wear chikan proudly, to remind yourself, to remind everyone around you, that legacy is important, that it is everything, that we are heathens if we cannot appreciate a centuries-old craft that speaks to art, beauty, knowledge and privilege.

And so it goes. Each city I visit, each country I wander around like a silly tourist, grabbing on to bits of information I gather from the people who walk its streets every day, informs me and my style. I probably look idiotic, showing up at work in my tailored Vietnamese silk dress one day and an Omani salwar-kameez the next, arriving at business meetings wearing three strands of pearls courtesy a Sri Lankan jeweller in Colombo, but in my mind, I know their meanings.

Everywhere I go, I wonder, could I live here? Is this where I was meant to be born and raised and schooled? Is this where I could end up someday, a happy expat, with beautiful, confused children? In my rings and dresses and shoes I carry memories of places and experiences that are otherwise impossible to share, to touch. Travel is so rich, and yet so fleeting, and perhaps the best way I know to truly immerse myself in a new culture, to try and understand it at its core, to taste and remember this new life, is to collect souvenirs, to wear them wherever I go.

So yes, I will sometimes waste my hard-earned money on an item that I will wear twice before feeling guilt pangs and realizing that it was a terribly foolish decision. Sometimes, I may stand in a freezing room and contemplate going against all my ethics, momentarily swept up in the beliefs and values of a foreign culture. But what is the point of travel—and fashion, and life in general—if you don't allow your mind to wander, and let yourself make some mistakes?

Jewel, the Clown

Abeer Y. Hoque

He learns to twist a camel out of balloons, a heart out of wood, a clown out of himself. His first job after returning to Berkeley is his favourite and not just because it lets him sleep till noon on most days. Black the shadows around his eyes, lush the paint on his lips, harlequin his suit. By turn, tranny and entrancing, fantastical and fickle, he plays his part like a pro. The mothers love him because he bows low over their outstretched hands, presses Day-Glo kisses into their palms.

Each house is a set, designed for his play, the backyard stages, the gardens, the hallways. A red-carpet entrance festooned with balloons, stars, the moon. The stairs to the front door are chalked with paisley designs, smudged at the edges by tiny shoe prints. Cobwebs of paper flowers hang high up in the eaves, Crayola and origami blossoms. And the bushes weep crepe streamers, fluttering, rustling, as he passes.

The least he can do is begin with a flourish.

'I'm Jewel, the clown,' he pronounces in that dream of children's parties, knowing no one will believe him.

The hostess looks up from mopping a spill or refilling a bowl of crunch pop cereal. 'And you're late,' she says, trying not to sound harried, folding out a ruffle on a red dress less worn.

'And you're looking beautiful.' His painted smile widens. 'Don't worry. The best is for the last.'

The clowning is a chance gig. He never thought he'd do anything like it, not so bodily, so in disguise. In the beginning, when he first comes back home to Berkeley, every day, he goes for a walk, to remind himself where he is. Not that this works for a place as dreamy as the East Bay in the summer. The air is so light around him that he can't be sure he's even breathing. *Like a jasper, clear as crystal.*

Down Telegraph, he hears a woman laughing inside a store, near his sister's old thrift store haunts, a warm wide sound. He stops at the window and looks in. A dark-skinned woman is pointing at something he can't see, her long hair in motion. It's a party store, a toy chest, floor to ceiling crammed with props and costumes and games. When he walks in, a jack in the box greets him in alarm, sending him sideways into a vampire display.

Recovering, he sees a clown wig that's been pulled from its package and abandoned on a shelf. He picks it up and its soft spotted shape collapses in his hands, an invitation. He's adjusting it on his head as the woman turns into the aisle he's standing in. She's South Asian, svelte and handsome, wearing a clinging maroon sweater dress. It makes her black hair look blacker. She's in mid-sentence but stops when he cocks his head and bows, undressing her in his mind, the dress peeling off like a revelation.

Straightening elaborately, he sees a small boy behind her, peering through her legs. He forgets about the mother. Thinking of another boy dancing, teardrop eyes and fawn skin, he picks up a crooked cane and three-steps closer, the music in his head a winnowing waltz. The boy's wet eyes widen, his mouth parts.

He whistles up the scale, flips the cane around like a majorette, and then whistles down. Losing control of his prop, he catches hold of it at its curve, his fingers clutching hard, and the stump end shoots out a flower. He mockingly falls over, startled, making them all laugh, including the store owner who has come around to stop and then watch his show.

After the woman has gone, he looks at the owner in apology. 'It was out of its box, the wig I mean. So I thought I'd try it on.'

The man is plump, ripe like a fruit, in a gingham suit slightly too small. He has a hesitating way, almost a stammer, something that he overcomes with an inhale and burst of words. 'Are you looking for an extra clowning gig? Because I need someone for some parties coming up.'

It's as if this is what he does for a living, as if a clown getup were just another day in Berkeley. Since he doesn't have any other living, he takes it up. He pats the wig and says, smiling, 'I got openings, sure.' And this is how it begins.

But something about being in costume changes him. He has never before had any desire to vamp or tease. In high school, everyone had a costume, a look, even the people who didn't. The dramatists, the rockers, the dropouts, the ballers, the artists, the wannabes, the schoolers, the schooled. His crew, the addicts, also put it on, but he had never been interested, wearing the same jeans weeks straight, the same jacket for years.

But now, he gets dressed up carefully at home and goes to these daylight parties, sunlight clearing his eyes. Every corner he turns turns him: cowboy outlaw for a block, sad mime for another, foreign prince, mad hatter, fairy.

At parties, he blows and twists balloon animals, hands out tiny carved wooden blocks, pulls out Nan's old magic tricks, coins from behind ears, handkerchiefs from sleeves, cards from pockets. He saves the music for last, pulling out his battered keyboard like a trophy, winks and begins. Magic how the mayhem, the fighters and the fleet-footed, all merge into one voice, sometimes harmonious, always sincere.

'Who wants to be the song king next?'

A clamour drowns him out and so he does what he always does. He pulls at his coiled and coloured hair as if in despair, and then with two trembling hands, he points at the smallest child. Another tumult.

'She can't be king.'

'She's too little!'

'She can't sing!'

'She's a girl!'

'Oh, we'll show them, won't we, doll?' He steadies his trembling hands for a hot minute. 'It's apple pie. Anyone can eat it. Eeeeeven a girrrrrrl...'

It saves him in the beginning, and for a long time after. It's the kids, as spoiled and shrieking as they are. They ooze love, spill it at the drop of a hat. It comes through the high class, the high maintenance, emerges on the other side undiminished. He wants it, needs it, hasn't known how much, until now.

'Jewel, tell us a story!'

'Sure, have I told you the one about the dealer?' he asks, sotto voce, feeling the mothers' eyes swivelling his way. 'Well, there was a little boy who was afraid of everything, of his own shadow sometimes. And this is the story of how he became so brave, they called him the Dealer, because he could deal ... with anything...' And the mothers' eyes swivel away.

He loves the earnestness. Nobody does earnest like a kid. Everyone else has context, backstory, agenda, as soon as they hit double digits, sometimes earlier. It's why he keeps doing it, even though over time, he can feel the disguises unmooring him, each one puppeteering a different identity, like a destructive tic, untying his characteristics from one another, letting them loose.

He knows he should quit but keeps on at it for longer than he wants, than he can bear, because of Oola. His daughter loves the wigs, the war paint, the whirling dervish music. He plans and puts on special shows for her, learns how to throw his voice, makes costumes for her so she can play along.

She's a natural, Oola is, with her wide eyes, open face. She inhabits the costumes in a way he can't. His opacity lends his performances a certain air, something that is his alone. He remains himself, some version or filter of the centre. Some of these versions can't live with each other, mad and jiggering as they are, so they stay hidden until there's space. In a way, the clowning lets them have their day, but underneath it all, it's him. Oola, on the other hand, disappears into the disguises chameleon-like. They become her, and she them. You might forget what she looked like before. Or maybe you never knew.

It's the getting home that gets him in the end and forces him out. The BART is distracting enough, rolling through West Oakland, skyscraper high, dinosaur cranes moving slowly through mountains of girders and freight. Too soon he is shaking with the effort to string together his personality, to become himself again, so he'll not scatter into a million pieces when Oola opens the door, barrels into him. Each of the blue and steel train cars contain a thousand of his hissed prayers, one line running to keep up with the last.

By the declining day

I swear by the time

Lo!

He calls and he waits, knowing the wanting is an answer in itself, but finding no peace in it. How long? How long?

Most surely man is in loss.

He can tell when it's starting, from his breathing, a tripping, a treason. He starts wearing headphones so he can try to remix the feeling with a music different than the one in his brain. Still, the panic reaches from his belly in all directions, like an animal hungry for the food of his body, caving his lungs for air, hollowing out his heart.

Save those who believe.

He starts waiting till dark, so Oola will be asleep by the time he's home, pacing in the station shadows, the thing growing with the darkness. It won't be till he fumbles home, locks himself in the bathroom, starts sponging off the make-up, that it will relent. He watches his face emerge from behind the paint, the lips thinning, the eyes receding, the hair deflating, the reduction of himself to himself.

Exhort one another to truth.

When the faces are gone from his face, only then will it curl up. When he finally falls asleep, his body exhausted of exhaustion, only then will it go to sleep.

Exhort one another to endure.

It's the mothers that he misses when he stops clowning. The children are still there, playing piano alongside him, everyone dressed in street clothes, corduroys and T-shirts and fleece. No more parachute pants, no more paint, panic no longer parked in his belly.

When the piano lessons take place in his house, he catches glimpses of the mothers, waving to him as the kids spill from old Volvos, new minivans. When he teaches in other houses, he hears the mothers' voices call from other rooms, requests, threats, endearments. He doesn't want that authority and affection directed towards him. He spent most of his childhood keeping out of his own mother's line of sight. But he likes watching it, like the old Westerns where you know it ends happily.

Still his old clown name follows him home. Jewel. He remembers the day Oola first says it. He doesn't know how but one morning when he wakes her up for school, she snuffles it secretly into his neck as he's carrying her to the bathroom. It was Mamma's pet name for him, the one he stopped answering to when he decided to stop being her pet, as if that were something he could do. He didn't understand then that the name was more than a name. He does now. It's why he lets Oola keep calling him Jewel. He figures what part of him got lost when Mamma lost him is what Oola found, for better and worse.

The shelf in the bathroom slowly gathers dust. He touches the pots of powder and paint, glitter falling from his fingertips to the floor. It's better this way: that only the name is what's left. In place of everything else, a child stands in the doorway, waiting to enter. He arranges his face into greeting, knowing it will settle into truth with one return grin. He flourishes towards the piano, bell bottoms swinging. He found these pants in a trunk older than him. He'd never have bought something so paisley, so pop, but it fits yesterday's clown, today's mood.

'Come, come! The bell jar of music awaits.' His ringmaster habit of catching and twisting words into ceremony holds yet.

'What's a bell jar?'

'Ah, don't you know...'

And the music fills the spaces if nothing else will.

THINGS TO THINK ABOUT WHEN YOU ARE BUYING CLOTHES

MEENA KANDASAMY

Trying to escape the poverty of life in a land where agriculture had dismally failed, where their hereditary profession of being nomadic witch-doctors no longer held any meaning in a modernizing society, all of my male cousins fled the village that my paternal grandparents had made their home. My father had run away from that landscape a generation before them, got a university education, married up and above his level. He had never looked back, because making-do in a city was difficult enough, but perhaps because of a fear that if he were to go back, he could never escape another time. I am a privileged child, I grew up in the city and I now live in London, I have no taste of that horror which my cousins experience. One half of them went to Malaysia to work as cooks in roadside eateries, the other migrated to Tirupur and Coimbatore to work in garment factories. My cousin works as a tailor there, doing the intricate, finishing job of sewing buttons, of doing the collars on male shirts—the kind of work that requires a fine eye and finer fingers. What can I claim to know about my cousin's life? To me, sewing is the leisurely pastime on a sunny day—it is a wrap-around skirt I make from a Size 12 summer dress, or cotton pillow covers I fashion out of very large Ikea curtains. I do not know the factory floor. I do not know sewing that will feed a family. I will never know the seventy-hour working week that will one day become the money that will marry off my sisters. I thought about this when I wanted to start writing this story, but could not get the courage to share. It is an aspect of my life I hide, and I hide it very well. More than that, it is only *personal* by extension, the pain is not my own, my cousin's poverty is not a wound that I can tend, or dress, or heal. And he is not alone.

1. Before I write of my cousin, before I wanted to bring in any personal touch to the story, I wrote about how clothing claims lives even before it is made. I started with the statistics: Thirty-one farmers kill themselves every day, and cotton farmers headline this list.[1] This is how shiny, glitzy neoliberalism brought death—farmers switched from food crops to cash crops in the dream of export-led growth. This suicide story is the tale of western India, a land where the skies bake the earth to yield the purest white clouds of cotton, this is the land that goes by the name of suicide belt. This is where Monsanto's genetically modified seeds, now used on about 90 per cent of India's cotton fields,[2] became, in the words of the renowned environmental activist Vandana

1. India's Union Agricultural Minister Radha Mohan Singh submitted the figure of 11,400 farmer suicides in the year 2016. The figures have been higher in previous years: 12,602 in the year 2015. News report accessible here: http://www.firstpost.com/india/11400-farmers-committed-suicide-in-2016-govt-tells-lok-sabha-3832577.html

2. This is a widely used statistic, including in this Reuters story here: 'Indian farmers cotton on to new seed, in blow to Monsanto', 3 August 2016 http://www.reuters.com/article/us-india-monsanto-idUSKCN10E05C

Shiva, the infamous 'suicide seeds'.[3] This is the land of loan-sharks; where the state eases itself into an afternoon siesta, where the rural banks have been shut down, where moneylenders convert wispy cotton into sturdy nooses as they watch debt-ridden farmers hang themselves. This is a land of young widows left to look after their little children; women who work for less than two dollars a day; kids who drop out when school becomes an unaffordable luxury. These are the fields that lay themselves bare to drought, to hailstones, to calamity—crop failure is one of the many unmourned victims of climate change.[4]

---

3. Most of the 300,000 farmer suicides in India since 1995 (when the WTO came into force) are concentrated in the cotton belt. And 95 per cent of the cotton in India is controlled by Monsanto. Source: Vandana Shiva, 'How Monstanto Wrote and Broke Laws to Enter India', Seed Freedom, 27 July 2015 http://seedfreedom.info/how-monsanto-wrote-and-broke-laws-to-enter-india/ Also, here's some background: Monsanto was only able to enter the market in 1988 when the World Bank gave India a $150 million loan to privatize its seed industry and deregulate it. While this helped bring better technology to India, it also disrupted the traditional ways farmers would save seeds and develop their own hybrids. Close to 90 per cent of the cotton grown in India today uses Monsanto's technology, which is licensed to forty-nine Indian seed companies. Indian patent laws prevent life forms from being patented, but Monsanto's seeds are genetically engineered and qualify for an exception. According to Reuters, 41 million GM cotton seed packets were sold last year, earning royalties of 6.5 billion Indian rupees ($97 million) for Monsanto. Read more: 'Monsanto's India Problem' (MON, BAYN.DE) | Investopedia http://www.investopedia.com/news/monsantos-india-problem-mon-baynde/#ixzz4oaCTprUJ

4. A study by the University of California at Berkeley has found a correlation between a 1 degree celsius rise in average temperature on any

2. When I think of cotton plantations, it conjures up the reek of sweat and the sound of whiplashes, the soul-crushing images of slavery and indenture. It is not history alone that holds us prisoner. I learn of how cotton subsidies in the West and the introduction of Monsanto seeds ate up the fields and the farmers in the African nations of Burkina Faso, Benin, Mali and Chad. I tell myself to not wander away, to not go global, to stick to home territory, to only tell the story of India because there are countless stories that need telling here. Most of all, because like every Indian story, caste entangles the story of clothes and clothing here.

3. In Vidarbha,[5] for instance, where there are 3.2 million farmers depending on cotton for a living, a farmer suicide is reported every eight hours. Producing more than 40 million bales of cotton a year[6] does not save India's farmers—

---

day in the growing season corresponding to sixty-seven more suicides. They argue that climate change could have contributed to the death of more than 60,000 farmers and farm workers in the last three decades in India: Accessible here: https://www.theguardian.com/environment/2017/jul/31/suicides-of-nearly-60000-indian-farmers-linked-to-climate-change-study-claims

5. For an engaging portrayal of the farmer suicides in Vidarbha, please watch the PBS 'Wide Angle' documentary, *The Dying Fields* (directed by Fred de Sam Lazaro, 2008). The 'a farmer commits suicide every eight hours' statistic is from the documentary, but is also quoted in this *New York Times* review: http://www.nytimes.com/2007/08/28/arts/television/28fiel.html

6. Projected estimate by the Cotton Association of India for the year 2016-17. Source: http://www.business-standard.com/article/markets/cai-projects-33-60-million-bales-cotton-production-for-2016-17-116083000417_1.html

the surplus pushes down the global prices, the success on the fields comes back to kill them. India's liberalization programme of throwing open its markets to foreign produce has not helped either: the suicides began at around the same time when Indian cotton farmers were forced to compete with farmers from other countries where agriculture is highly subsizidized. Yet, it's not the farmers alone who suffer. The Rumpelstiltskins—the weavers who spin this white gold into coarse cloth—face bleak futures too.

4. Sometimes, to report on the starvation deaths and the soup kitchens that have become the plight of the weavers and their families, the news media indulge in clothing-related puns. 'Looming disaster' is a perennial favourite.

5. Failure appears to be the fate of the working class. Indian handloom, with its quaintness, its earthiness, its authenticity lends itself to designer dreams. The fashion industry cannibalizes a craft, a culture and artisanal castes. The weavers who hand-spin these dreams battle a poverty they cannot escape.[7]

---

7. In my home state of Tamil Nadu, I remember vividly that in the last decade weavers have been pushed to the brink of poverty and starvation. Beginning in 2002, both major parties in the state (the DMK and the AIADMK) have competed with each other to open *kanchi thotti* 'gruel centers' (soup kitchens) where these starving weavers could have a meal—and charity organizations, welfare organizations, churches, religious establishments have also followed suit to try and mitigate their difficulty. For more information, see this story in *Frontline* 'Weavers in Distress', dated 17 August 2002, accessible here: http://www.frontline.in/static/html/fl1917/19171250.htm For a recent story, refer to this *Times of India* (25 April 2016) report on the cotton weavers of the state where you

6. Propaganda is central to everything, so allow me to corrupt your clean minds with some words from *The Poverty of Philosophy*. Marx wrote: 'In acquiring new productive forces men change their mode of production; and in changing their mode of production, in changing the way of earning their living, they change all their social relations. The hand-mill gives you society with the feudal lord; the steam-mill society with the industrial capitalist.'[8]

In the country that I'm writing about, the land that this essay tries to lay threadbare, there are hand-mills and power looms, the feudal lords and the industrial capitalists, all existing side by side.

7. In India, with its caste system, even Marx—so straight, so white—has to retreat into the margins to watch how it is *not* the modes of production that change social relations, but how it is the social relations that superimpose themselves and work their way around the modes of production. Caste reproduced itself successfully within the dominion of capitalism. Dalit men worked in the poorly paid ring-spinning departments of the textile mills (they constituted 40 per cent of the male workforce there), whereas the more lucrative weaving sheds, with the highest paid skilled workers,

---

encounter a picture of people leaving the weaving profession to sell newspapers because of acute poverty. Accessible here: http://blogs.timesofindia.indiatimes.com/tracking-indian-communities/tamil-nadu-cotton-weaves-on-wane-get-a-boost/

8. Karl Marx, *The Philosophy of Poverty*, accessed from the Marxists Internet Archive: https://www.marxists.org/archive/marx/works/subject/hist-mat/pov-phil/ch02.htm, 8 July 2017

were closed to them (they had a dismal representation there: 0.6 per cent).[9] Dalit women, thrice oppressed by caste, class and gender, were largely relegated to the winding and reeling department. The advent of technology did not crush caste, it only created new roles, new segmentations of labour. Where the pay itself did not vary, and was equal to all labourers within a department—the work areas were segregated, with no mixing of the caste-Hindus and the Dalits, and that was how untouchability was maintained. This was the reciprocal bounty of capitalism—to respect caste, to sustain caste, to structure itself around the boundary walls of the caste system.

8. How could cruelty be far behind once caste and capitalism came some place? It was not a mere coincidence that the most accident-prone areas of the mill, like the throstle department, were the places that employed the most Dalits.[10]

---

9. 'By 1921, 12 per cent of the workforce of the Bombay mills was Untouchable. As in the railways, Untouchables were concentrated in the least preferred sectors of the mills. Over 72 per cent of Untouchable men were in the ring-spinning department, where they comprised 40 per cent of total male workers and were almost comprehensively shut out of the higher-status and better-paid weaving department.' Source: Morris David Morris, *The Emergence of an Industrial Labour Force in India: A Study of the Bombay Cotton Mills 1854-1947*, University of California Press, 1965 (pp. 75-79) as quoted in Mendelsohn and Vicziany, *The Untouchables: Subordination, Poverty and the State in Modern India*, Cambridge University Press, 1998, p. 89.

10. Original quote: 'In those days many accidents used to occur in the throstle departments of mills and workers considered them very unsafe to work there. Since workers from upper castes usually did not agree to

9. Was it a question of economics or safety alone that relegated the Dalits to the lowest rungs of the textile mills? No, it was caste with its ideas of pollution and purity too. Let me quote Jan Breman paraphrasing Salim Lakha:[11] 'The work in the mills was determined by the caste identity which the workers had brought with them to city. Dheds and Vankars, who had supplemented their income from farm labour by weaving, were put to work in the spinning shops, as were the Chamars, a leather-tanning caste. These untouchables were not admitted to the weaving shops, which were a domain of the Muslims and of higher castes like the Kanbis. This division of labour, which developed towards the end of the nineteenth century, was justified on the basis that weavers needed both hands and their mouth to tie a knot in the thread if it broke or to suck the yarn onto the shuttle whenever a weft bobbin was replaced. If members of the untouchable castes were permitted to do this work, it would defile the resulting product. This pollution would be passed on to the subsequent stages of production. To avoid this, the untouchables were only eligible for the preceding phase of spinning.' The saliva of some people was permissible,

---

working in them, they were spared for the untouchable worker.' Paresh Majmundar: *An Anatomy of Peaceful Industrial Relations*, N.M. Tripathi Publishers, 1973, p. 120, digital archives from the University of Michigan (2008), quoted in *Jan Breman, The Making and Unmaking of an Industrial Working Class*, Amsterdam University Press, 2004, p. 18.

11. Salim Lakha, *Capitalism and Class in Colonial India: The Case of Ahmedabad*, Sterling Publishers, 1988, pp. 87-8, quoted in Breman, *The Making and Unmaking of an Industrial Working Class*, ibid, p. 17.

of some people was polluting. That is how Dalits pushed out of the villages by failing agriculture, running away from feudal oppression and chasing their big-city dreams found themselves in the capitalist framework: in the spinning shops, and working where the raw cotton was delivered and stored. To quote Breman, again, 'The division of tasks in the mills closely, if not entirely, followed the hierarchy of the caste system.'[12]

10. The shop floors alone did not enforce caste—it worked its way through the entire industrial complex. The caste-Hindu workers ate inside the canteens, the Dalit workers outside. An untouchable worker who claimed to be a Muslim to get work in the weaving department was severely beaten when it was revealed that he was a Mahar.[13] The water tanks for the caste-Hindus and the Dalits were separate. Untouchability was rampant in these mills, as it was everywhere.

11. To pause to breathe, let us remember the revolutionary words of Dr Ambedkar, 'Caste is not merely a division of labour, it is a division of labourers.'

---

12. Jan Breman, *The Making and Unmaking of an Industrial Working Class: Sliding Down the Labour Hierarchy in Ahmedabad, India*, Amsterdam University Press, 2004, p. 131.

13. Dr Ambedkar's evidence before the Southborough Committee (1919) which was one of his first political engagements—what we have is a transcript of his deposition from the records which reads as follows: 'In the mills in the Bombay Presidency the untouchables were not yet allowed to work in the weaving department: in one case an untouchable did work in the weaving department of a mill saying that he was a Mohammedan, and when found out, he was severely beaten.' Dr Babasaheb Ambedkar: *Writings and Speeches*, Volume 1, p. 274. Accessible online here: https://www.mea.gov.in/Images/attach/amb/Volume_01.pdf

12. Did trade unionism break caste, did it erase these discriminations, did it unite the workers who had nothing to lose but their chains?

In the historic 1928 textile workers strike that shut down all the mills in Bombay, Dr Ambedkar supported the communists in the strike on the ground that trade unions would recognize the right of the Dalits to work in all the departments. What was the reaction to this demand? In his own words, 'They afterwards consented, most reluctantly, to include this as one of their demands, and when they presented this to the millowners, the millowners very rightly snubbed them and said that if this was an injustice, they certainly were not responsible for it.' The following year, Dr Ambedkar would call upon the Dalit workers to not take part in the strikes, to stress upon their discriminated position in the workforce, and because it was economically unviable for the Dalits to strike when they were at the mercy of moneylenders. Caste became a fault line within the class struggle, and all of this history is woven across the history of textile in India.

13. Allow me the temptation to smuggle in something in the question-and-answer format to shed some light on the issue of untouchability in the textile mills of Bombay. When I was looking for information, or what passes off as research–I found these little treasures in an unlikely place: in Dr Ambedkar's evidence before the Indian Statuory Commission (more popularly known as the Simon Commission, consisting of a team of seven British Parliamentarians sent to the country to examine constitutional affairs) dating from October 1928.

I present before you three excerpts of his submissions before the Commission:[14]

Exhibit One:

Q. Major [Clement] Attlee: Are there members of the depressed classes working in industry, in the cotton mills and so on?

Dr Ambedkar: All of them. The depressed class men are all labourers.

Q. You have not got my point; I am talking of industry. You have members of the depressed classes who work in villages, for the most part in certain occupations. But are there large numbers of the depressed classes engaged in industry?

Dr Ambedkar : A very large number.

Q. You would have a very large number in a place like Bombay City?

Dr Ambedkar: Yes.

Q. Do they cease in any degree to be untouchable?

Dr Ambedkar: No, I should like to point out this. The depressed class man is entirely kept out of the weaving department, the most paying department. He can only enter departments like the throstle department and others.

---

14. Dr Ambedkar, 'Evidence Before the Simon Commission', retrieved from: https://archive.org/stream/Ambedkar_CompleteWorks/14D.%20Dr.%20Ambedkar%20with%20the%20Simon%20Commission%20D_djvu.txt, accessed on 1 August 2017

Q. Why?

Dr Ambedkar: On account of untouchability.

Q. When he is working there he is working alongside people of all castes?

Dr Ambedkar : Not quite. The departments are discriminated according to castes. One department is entirely manned by the depressed classes; another—say the weaving department—by Mohammedans and caste Hindus.

Q. Do they take part in the trade unions?

Dr Ambedkar: Yes, they are beginning to do so.

Q. With members of the classes above the depressed classes?

Dr Ambedkar: Yes.

Q. I wanted to get this point from you. You put forward a claim for representation of the depressed classes on the basis of numbers. Now, we have claims put forward on a different basis altogether; on, say, the labour basis. You get a cross-division in that way, because a man can be a depressed class man and he can also be a labourer?

Dr Ambedkar: He is usually, if not always, a labourer.

*

Exhibit Two:

Q. May I revert to a question put to you by Major Attlee? I gather the depressed classes work in the factories in isolation?

Dr Ambedkar: In isolation, yes.

Q. They have their own shed and their own department?

Dr Ambedkar: Their own department; there are no sheds.

Q. Whatever it is, they are separated from the other workers in the factory?

Dr Ambedkar: I would rather put it in this way, that certain departments are exclusively assigned to the depressed classes and certain departments are departments into which they are not allowed to enter.

Q. Certain kinds of occupations are forbidden to them?

Dr Ambedkar: In the mills, yes.

Q. I think you said they are not allowed to go into the weaving department?

Dr Ambedkar: Yes.

Q. If they became members of the same trade union, would the workers in the weaving department decline to allow them in?

Dr Ambedkar: They would decline to allow them in. If I may mention one thing, in the recent Bombay strike this matter was brought up prominently by me. I said to the members of the union that if they did not recognize the right of the depressed classes to work all the departments, I would rather dissuade the depressed classes from taking part in the strike. They afterwards consented, most reluctantly, to include this as one of their demands, and when they presented this to the millowners, the millowners very rightly snubbed them and said that if this was an injustice, they certainly were not responsible for it.

Q. It is not altogether merely a case of the employers wanting to get cheap labour and confining certain departments to the depressed classes for economic reasons?

Dr Ambedkar: No, it is untouchability.

Q. Would there be anything of this in the situation? The better-paid Indian, say, declines to allow the untouchable to come into his department for fear that the effect of their lower wages would be to depress wages in his department?

Dr Ambedkar: No. There is no distinction on the basis of wages.

Q. That does not come into it at all?

Dr Ambedkar: No, not at all.

Q. It is merely a question of untouchability?

Dr Ambedkar: Quite so.

*

Exhibit Three:

Q. Mr Premchand: Do you know the depressed classes are employed in the weaving departments of the Ahmedabad mills?

Dr Ambedkar: I did not know that.

Q. I can tell you they are.

Dr Ambedkar: There again I should like to say one thing, probably they are employed exclusively. I can quite conceive of a situation where, for instance, so many looms are exclusively handed over to the depressed classes. Today there is a proposal also in certain mills that the depressed classes should take charge of the whole of the weaving department, that the millowners should hand it over to them, but you cannot have part depressed classes and part caste Hindus.

Q. Chairman: The difficulty is the mixture?

Dr Ambedkar: Yes.

*

14. This was a story of exclusion and discrimination that did not belong to Bombay alone, but had taken place everywhere else in India. In 1918, a year after the Russian Revolution, India had its first trade union: Madras Labour Union formed by mill-workers at the Buckingham and Carnatic Mills who worked under extremely exploitative circumstances. In 1921, when the mill-workers at the Buckingham and Carnatic Mills went on strike from June to October, crippling the Madras economy, the Dalit workers, facing starvation and lacking the social capital of caste-Hindu workers, were forced by circumstances to go back to work. To pull them into line, and using the ruse of attacking scab workers, caste-Hindus burnt a 100 huts of Dalit workers in Pulianthope on 28 June 1921. Because caste stayed in control of the narrative, it would conveniently present Dalit workers as strike-breakers; vilify and erase their militancy, and rob them of being recognized for their sacrifices in the working-class movements.[15]

15. For an in-depth and meaningful account of early trade unionism in Madras, as well as the issues of caste/untouchability, the role of the political movements and parties of that time, do read D.Veeraraghavan's book *The Making of the Madras Working Class* (Leftword, 2013).

15. Caste is about those who spin and those who weave and those who make the clothes. Caste is about touch and caste is about spit. Caste is about exploitative baniyas who own these mills, it is about who is allowed to work where. Long before capitalism enters this scene of crime, caste had other rules. About wearing clothes, about not wearing clothes, about how to wear clothes and about washing clothes. There is nothing that is beyond the pale of regimentation by the caste system.

16. Stripping a Dalit is one of the most recurrent caste atrocities that occur in our country. To quote from the Scheduled Caste and Scheduled Tribe (Prevention of Atrocities) Act, it is an atrocity when a caste-Hindu forcibly removes clothes from the person of a member of a Scheduled Caste or a Scheduled Tribe or parades them naked or with painted face or body or commits any similar act which is derogatory to human dignity. As an everyday horror show, it finds its ways into headlines because it couples dominance with the predatory gaze. Dalit men and women are stripped and/or paraded naked when they do not follow caste diktats.

17. Sometimes, the rules about clothes extend to things that are not clothes, but accessories nonetheless. Dalits, in many villages in Tamil Nadu, were prohibited from wearing shoes or sandals, draping a towel on their shoulders, unfurling their umbrellas, riding cycles or motorcycles on caste-Hindu streets. A Dalit would have to pick up his footwear when he trod through these streets, he would have to tuck his towel or his umbrella under his armpit, he would have to alight from

his bicycle and push it through. In this manner, the vicious ego of caste oppression gloats, unwilling to accept the change that is sweeping through society.

18. In the militant village of Kilvenmani, an elderly Dalit farm-worker told me of the time he had worn a red shirt to school—and his teacher had called him 'Danger' and sent him back home. In Tamil Nadu, self-respect became synonymous with the Black Shirt of the Dravidian movement. Sometimes, self-respect became synonymous with any shirt. All through my childhood, I've heard variations of this from my own father: 'I could wear a shirt because of Periyar.' A shirt served as a symbol of aspiration to equality, and more than that, a claim to what one deserved in place of being consigned to nothing.

19. Periyar E.V. Ramasamy (1879–1973) may have been responsible for millions of men like my father gaining the right to wear shirts or go to school or enter college, but most of all, he will be remembered for telling women to step out of the constraints of the many-yards sari, telling them to dress in shirts and trousers, telling them to cut their hair short, telling them to be equal to men in everything.

20. Periyar was not the only anti-caste leader who addressed the question of clothing in a caste society. When caste made rules to distinguish between the touchables and untouchables through material markers, it was the work of revolutionaries to turn the tide. Dr Ambedkar addressing Dalit women in the Mahad conference in 1928, said, 'Untouchables do not have a stamp of their Untouchable status on their foreheads.

But Untouchables can be immediately identified due to their ways of living which I think have been forced upon us. Hence you should abandon all markers that will identify you as Untouchables. Your style of draping saris is one such marker. You should destroy this evidence. You should make it a habit to drape saris like the high-caste women. Similarly, the many necklaces and silver and tin bangles up to your elbow are also a mark of identification. [...] Change your sari-draping style before you go home.'[16]

21. And they did. Shailaja Paik writes, 'Immediately after his Mahad speech, helped by the radical upper-caste women Lakshmibai Tipnis and Indirabai Chitre from the Chandraseniya Kayastha Prabhu community, women readily draped their saris like upper-caste women, covering their legs down to their ankles.'[17] Under an oppressive system that demarcated who should wear what, dress lends itself to rebellion, and to camouflage. Dr Ambedkar would touch upon clothes again, exhorting Dalit women to wear white saris on 14 October 1956, the day on which he and close to half a million followers embraced Buddhism, refusing to die as Untouchables under a horrendous caste system.

22. Not always did men, male reformers, have to lead the struggle against caste in the matter of clothing. In a

---

16. Dr Ambedkar writing in the *Bahishkrut Bharat*, 3 February 1928, quoted in Shailaja Paik, *Dalit Women's Education in Modern India: Double Discrimination*, Routledge Research on Gender in Asia Series, 2014.

17. Paik, ibid.

society where stripping Dalits of their clothes is a form of punishment, dress becomes a form of resistance.

In the nineteenth century, Nadar (or Chaanar) women, of the caste of toddy-tappers, prohibited from wearing jackets or blouses to cover their upper bodies in the style of upper-caste women lead a successful revolt against the Travancore kingdom. This phenomenal struggle took place at the confluence of various strands of history, which also involved the church, conversions and British colonial authority.[18]

Another exemplary incident of individual rebellion is the story of Nangeli, who refused to pay the *mulakkaram*, a tax that Dalit women had to pay in the nineteenth century to the government of the Travancore Kingdom for covering their breasts. When the tax-collectors came knocking at her door, she chopped her breast and offered it on a plantain leaf, dying shortly thereafter.[19] It is in these snippets of our history that we realize how bloody and how brutal the caste system was and remains, and how clothes (neutral, beautiful, innocent) have been at the centre of so much control.

---

18. For more information on this revolt (also known as the *Maru Marakkal Samaram*), read: Eliza Kent, *Converting Women: Gender and Protestant Christianity in Colonial South India*, Oxford University Press, 2004; Robert Hardgrave, *The Nadars of Tamilnad: The Political Culture of a Community in Change*, University of California Press, 1969. More particularly, the chapter 'Cloth, Clothes and Colonialism' in Bernard S. Cohn's book *Colonialism and its Forms of Knowledge: The British in India* (Princeton University Press, 1996), provides valuable background and knowledge.

19. 'The woman who cut off her breasts to protest a tax', 28 July 2016. Accessed from: http://www.bbc.co.uk/news/world-asia-india-36891356

23. Remember. Remember, even though I extend examples from history, this is a story of the here and now, of today.

24. In 2012, three hundred homes of Dalits in three villages in the Dharmapuri district were burnt down to express indignation over the inter-caste marriage of a Dalit man Ilavarasan and a Vanniyar woman Divya. The leader of Pattali Makkal Katchi (PMK), a Vanniyar Party renowned for its history of anti-Dalit violence, said, 'Dalit boys are wearing jeans, T-shirts and sunglasses and taking our girls away...'[20] An aspiration to style became the reason for a caste-based demonisation and a witch-hunt. Think of this when you slip into your T-shirt and jeans today.

20. 'Ramadoss consolidates intermediate caste groups against Dalits': Report in *The Hindu*, B. Kolappan, Chennai, 2 December 2012. Accessed from: http://www.thehindu.com/news/national/tamil-nadu/Ramadoss-consolidates-intermediate-caste-groups-against-Dalits/article12432099.ece

Contributors

Amitav Ghosh is the internationally bestselling author of *Sea of Poppies* (shortlisted for the Man Booker Prize) and *River of Smoke*, the first two novels in *The Ibis Trilogy*, of which *Flood of Fire* is the final instalment. He has written ten other novels and works of non-fiction, including three essay collections. A frequent contributor to *The New Yorker*, *The New Republic*, *The New York Times*, and others, his work has been translated into more than twenty languages. He currently divides his time between Calcutta, Goa and Brooklyn.

Moni Mohsin was born and raised in Lahore, Pakistan. She is a freelance journalist and author of two novels, the prize-winning *The End of Innocence* and *Duty Free*. Her bestselling collection of satirical columns, *The Dairy of a Social Butterfly* and *Return of the Butterfly*, are based on her long-running column for the Pakistani paper *The Friday Times*. She is married with two children and lives between London and Lahore.

Samanth Subramanian is a writer and journalist based in Dublin. His second book, *This Divided Island: Stories from the Sri Lankan War*, won the Crossword Non-Fiction Prize and was shortlisted for the Samuel Johnson Prize and the Royal Society of Literature's Ondaatje Prize. He has written for *The New Yorker*, *The New York Times*, *Guardian*, *Granta* and *WIRED*.

Kyung-Sook Shin is one of South Korea's most widely read novelists. She is the author of seven novels, including *The Girl Who Wrote Loneliness*, *I'll Be Right There* and *Please Look After Mom*, which was a *New York Times* bestseller, translated into more than thirty-five languages, and the winner of the Man Asian Literary Prize. Shin is the first Korean woman to receive this award.

Young-Lahn Chung is a translator based in Seoul. She teaches at Ewha Womans University.

Plum Sykes was born in London and educated at Oxford. She is a contributing editor at American *Vogue* and has written two bestselling novels, *Bergdorf Blondes* and *The Debutante Divorcée*. Her third novel, comic murder mystery, *Party Girls Die in Pearls*, has just been published.

Tishani Doshi writes essays, poetry and fiction. For fifteen years, she worked as a dancer with the Chandralekha troupe. She lives in Chennai and her latest book is a collection of poems, *Girls Are Coming Out of the Woods*.

Kanishk Tharoor is the author of a collection of short stories, *Swimmer Among the Stars*, which won the Tata First Book Award for Fiction. This New York-based author is also the presenter and writer of the BBC radio series Museum of Lost Objects. His essays have appeared in *The New York Times*, *Guardian*, *Nation*, *The New Yorker*, and elsewhere. He is a columnist for *The Hindu Business Line* and the *Hindustan Times*.

Jhumpa Lahiri is the author of four works of fiction: *Interpreter of Maladies*, *The Namesake*, *Unaccustomed Earth*, and *The Lowland*; and a work of non-fiction, *In Other Words*. She has received numerous awards, including the Pulitzer Prize; the PEN/Hemingway Award; the Frank O'Connor International Short Story Award; the Premio Gregor von Rezzori; the DSC Prize for South Asian Literature; a 2014 National Humanities Medal, awarded by President Barack Obama; and the Premio Internazionale Viareggio-Versilia, for *In Altre Parole*.

Ann Goldstein is an editor at *The New Yorker*. She has translated an incredibly diverse range of authors, among them Leopardi, Pier Paolo Pasolini, Elena Ferrante, Alessandro Piperno, Primo Levi and Alessandro Baricco.

Molly Crabapple is a New York-based artist, journalist and author of the memoir, *Drawing Blood*. She has drawn in and reported from Guantanamo Bay, Abu Dhabi's migrant labour camps, and in Syria, Lebanon, Gaza, the West Bank, and Iraqi Kurdistan. Crabapple is a contributing editor for *VICE*, and has written for publications including *The New York Times*, the *Paris Review* and *Vanity Fair*. Her work is in the permanent collection of the Museum of Modern Art.

Chandrahas Choudhury is the author of the novel *Arzee the Dwarf* and editor of the anthology *India: A Traveller's Literary Companion*. He is based in New Delhi.

Janice Pariat is the author of *Boats on Land: A Collection of Short Stories* and *Seahorse: A Novel*. She was awarded the Young Writer Award from the Sahitya Akademi and the Crossword Book Award for

Fiction in 2013. Most recently, she has published a novella *The Nine-Chambered Heart* which is being translated for publication into eight languages. Currently, she lives in New Delhi with a cat of many names.

Rosalyn D'Mello is a New Delhi-based freelance writer. She is the author of *A Handbook for My Lover*, an erotic memoir. She is a regular contributor to *Mint Lounge*, *Vogue*, *Midday*, *OPEN* magazine and *First Post*. She was the editor-in-chief of BLOUIN ARTINFO India, and a nominee for Forbes' Best Emerging Art Writer Award in 2014.

Vladimir Lucien is a writer and critic from Saint Lucia. His work has been published in several international journals and has been translated into Dutch, Italian and Mandarin. His debut collection of poetry, *Sounding Ground*, won the 2015 OCM Bocas Prize for Caribbean Literature. He is one of the most significant voices in Caribbean literature today.

Vayu Naidu received Europe's first doctorate in oral traditions and performance storytelling from the University of Leeds 1994. She was the first sage-in-residence at Eton College in 2013. Her novel *Sita's Ascent* was nominated for the Commonwealth Book Award. Her second novel is *The Sari of Surya Vilas*. Working with classical and contemporary music orchestras with storytelling, she is now research associate at SOAS, University of London.

Manu Joseph is a novelist, most recently of *Miss Laila, Armed and Dangerous*. His widely acclaimed novels, *Serious Men* and *The Illicit Happiness of Other People*, have been translated into many languages, and nominated for several prizes. Among other honours he is the winner of The Hindu Literature Prize and The American Pen Open Book Award. Based in New Delhi, he is among India's most popular commentators, and is a former columnist for *The New York Times*.

Divia Thani is the editor-in-chief of *Condé Nast Traveller*, as well as the Make in India magazine. She was formerly features editor at *Vogue* India. Divia spent her growing years between Mumbai and Lagos. She graduated summa cum laude with a degree in English from the University of Pittsburgh, where she won a Brackenridge fellowship as well as the Robert C. Laing award for excellence in creative writing.

Abeer Y. Hoque is a Nigerian-born Bangladeshi–American writer and photographer. She likes batik, making lists, and eyeliner on boys. Her books include *The Long Way Home*, a travel photography and poetry monograph (2013), *The Lovers and the Leavers*, a collection of linked stories, poems and photographs (2015) and *Olive Witch*, a memoir (2017). 'Jewel, the Clown' is an excerpt from her novel in progress.

Meena Kandasamy is a poet and novelist currently based in London. Her latest novel is *When I Hit You: Or, The Portrait of the Writer as a Young Wife*. She was a Charles Wallace India Fellow at the University of Kent, and has previously published two collections of poetry, *Touch* (2006) and *Ms Militancy* (2010) and a novel, *The Gypsy Goddess* (2014).

Sara Singh has drawn for as long as she can remember. Her watercolour and ink illustrations, fluid and ethereal, draw upon her intrigue for the human body. In addition to *Vogue*, Sara has collaborated with Cartier, Givenchy, Lillet, Bergdorf Goodman, and Tiffany & Co. She holds a degree in Fashion Design from Beckman's College of Design, and has lived in London, Stockholm and Florida. She currently resides in New York City.